SUCCESSFUL CAREER WOMEN

Successful Career Women

Their Professional and Personal Characteristics

Cecilia Ann Northcutt

Contributions in Women's Studies, Number 120

GREENWOOD PRESS
New York • Westport, Connecticut • London

Library of Congress Cataloging-in-Publication Data

Northcutt, Cecilia Ann.
  Successful career women : their professional and personal
characteristics / Cecilia Ann Northcutt.
    p. cm. — (Contributions in women's studies, ISSN 0147-104X ;
no. 120)
  Includes bibliographical references and index.
  ISBN 0-313-27256-5 (lib. bdg. : alk. paper)
  1. Women executives—Psychology. 2. Success—Psychological
aspects. 3. Career development—Psychological aspects. I. Title.
II. Series.
HD6054.3.N67   1991
305.43′658—dc20   90-38415

British Library Cataloguing in Publication Data is available.

Library of Congress Catalog Card Number: 90-38415
ISBN: 0-313-27256-5
ISSN: 0147-104X

First published in 1991

Greenwood Press, 88 Post Road West, Westport, CT   06881
An imprint of Greenwood Publishing Group, Inc.

Printed in the United States of America

The paper used in this book complies with the
Permanent Paper Standard issued by the National
Information Standards Organization (Z39.48-1984).

10 9 8 7 6 5 4 3 2 1

Contents

Tables

Acknowledgments

Many people have contributed in various ways to the completion of this work. I would like to express my appreciation to all of my "teachers," both those in formal education and those in life education. They include Dr. Betty Newlon, Dr. Oscar Christensen, Dr. Phil Lauver, Dr. Mary Wetzel, Dr. Richard Erickson, Margaret Dykinga, and my board group.

I am grateful for a most special person, my husband Sam, who encouraged me and helped when asked. His unfaltering belief in me provided vitally significant support during the writing of this book.

Eleanor and Kevin Peirce provided invaluable assistance by reading and critiquing the manuscript. I thank them both.

The career women who pioneered have created possibilities for other women. I offer them my gratitude and appreciation, for I now have a better understanding of their personal sacrifices. Finally, to the career women who so willingly gave of their time and expertise to provide the information on which this book is based, I express my heartfelt thanks.

SUCCESSFUL
CAREER
WOMEN

Chapter 1

Introduction

Women's participation in the labor force in this country has increased dramatically in the past few decades and has prompted much interest among researchers, particularly among those concerned with women, careers, and career development. Their research expanded the scope of information about women and careers. It ranged from how women's career development differs from men's, through the effects of differences in early socializing on career choices, to attitudes toward success as influenced by gender. The research examined how successful women are different from or similar to successful men by identifying some of the characteristics of success for women managers. Likewise, it considered how successful career women differ from or resemble both college women and homemakers. Generally, the earlier research has been very specific in its focus and has tended to compare successful career women with other groups.

While a broad range of topics relating to women and work has been studied, few defining characteristics have been established for successful career women in general. This lack may derive from the limited information available about the successful career woman across all levels (that is, entry, tenured, middle management, upper management, and executive positions) and fields.

Current labor market information reveals that the growing number of working women shows no indication of decreasing. In the past 30 years, the American labor force has been drastically changed by the increased employment of women. Not only do more women work outside of the home, but they are working in almost every field of employment (Bureau of Labor Statistics 1983). The sharpest sustained increase in women's participation in the work force has taken place since World War II. In 1947, women comprised 32 percent of the labor force; this increased to 43 percent in 1951 and to 51 percent in 1980 (Brown 1981, 14). By 1986, women's labor force participation stood at 55 percent (Bloom 1986). Given these figures and the fact that women are "latecomers" to the career and labor force, it is important and appropriate that women have access to any information that will assist them in their career success.

It is not surprising that most research comparisons on women's career success in the past have been made using the male model for *characteristics of success*. This model includes using predominantly high-status criteria, such as income, executive position, and power, to define success. Several studies have focused on females in male-dominated professions. One example, a study by Harlan and Weiss, compared a matched set of 50 male and 50 female managers who were employed in two retailing organizations. They found a great deal of similarity between the two groups:

Men and women were found to have very similar psychological profiles of high power and achievement needs, high self-esteem, and to be highly motivated to manage. In addition, both men and women experienced difficulty in understanding and planning their careers; obtaining balanced and useful feedback; and obtaining opportunities for new skill development. (cited in Brown 1981, 19)

The traits mentioned are some of the basic characteristics of success based on the male model of success. How might the characteristics of success differ for successful career women as a group? In other words, is there a definable female model of success?

Since women have "come late" to the labor market and have often combined their career with the primary responsibility for the home, it becomes obvious that their career development is going to be different from that of men. Because women have a more varied career development pattern than do men, it seems reasonable that career women may have more characteristics in common with each other than they do with men. If these characteristics could be identified, they could prove more valuable than those characteristics that women either do or do not share with men.

In addition to a different career development pattern, women have had a different socialization process which affects both their career choices and career development. Halcomb (1979, 7) sums up the problem of women finding success in their careers by stating: "Our ability to make it in the mainstream is blocked by both our inner conflicts and outer obstacles. We need to understand ourselves better in terms of the game that's being played. . . . We need to know *How women do it* [succeed]."

There has been considerable research on women and careers. The bulk of it has focused on (1) comparing women with men; (2) isolating specific groups of career women (physicians, lawyers, or executives being the most often used); (3) comparing specific groups of career women with homemakers; and (4) examining women in male-dominated or "nontraditional" careers.

What about other career women—those who are successful in business, education, or the arts, for example? What about the career women who are not mid-level or top-level managers, who earn less than $50,000, and who still feel successful in their careers? Are there characteristics and/or patterns that are shared by successful career women across career fields and across career levels? If research results are to be extrapolated to career women in general, then the whole spectrum of women in careers must be studied.

This study identifies the personal characteristics that successful career women have in common across career fields; considers differences in achievement/motivation and self-esteem between occupational fields, as well as other independent variables; provides demographic profiles of successful career women in general; and contributes to the general body of knowledge about women and careers.

In order to identify the characteristics and other specific information about successful career women in general, it is necessary to address the following questions:

1. Are there characteristics that successful career women have in common, regardless of their career fields? Are there characteristics specific to successful career women within given career fields? In terms of shared characteristics, does it make a difference whether women are working in female-dominated or male-dominated fields?

2. What factors affect women's self-esteem and achievement/ motivation? Do the levels of achievement/motivation and self-esteem of successful career women differ across occupational fields? Between ordinal (birth order) positions or ethnic groups? Does the income level or career level (management versus nonmanagement) of the career woman affect her level of achievement/motivation or self-esteem?

3. Other factors may also affect the self-esteem and achievement/motivation of successful career women. Is there a relationship between self-esteem and achievement/motivation, on the one hand, and the variable of age on the other; that is, will younger women have different levels from older women? What of individual perceptions of success? Do those who define success in financial terms have a different level of self-esteem or achievement/motivation from those who do not? Is there a relationship between the level of self-esteem and achievement/motivation and the degree to which career women feel satisfied with their financial compensation? Is there a relationship between their self-esteem and achievement/motivation and the degree to which they feel emotional satisfaction from their work?

4. What factors of self-esteem and achievement/motivation are shared by successful career women?

5. Do successful career women rank themselves as successful? How do they describe themselves?

6. What are the three major components of success as defined by this population? How do they define success in general? Does the definition differ by occupational grouping?

For the purposes of this study, the following definitions are used:

Successful career woman: a woman who has been recognized as successful by her peers, by virtue of having been either nominated for recognition or selected by a professional organization, civic group, women's recognition event, or her employer.

Self-esteem: self-image, an attitude that includes facts, opinions, and values with regard to self, as well as a favorable or unfavorable orientation toward self (Rosenberg 1965, 5).

Achievement/motivation: the propensity of individuals to desire achievement and/or to act on their desire to achieve.

This study rests on the following assumptions:

1. *Public recognition is a major component of success.*
   The literature indicates that recognition in some form is one of the indications of a successful person. Blotnick (1985) states that "Social beings that humans are, they want their labors to be recognized and rewarded by others."
   Individual Psychology, the personality theory of Alfred Adler (1870-1937) maintains that all behavior occurs in a social context and "sees individuals constantly in the process of striving" (Manaster and Corsini 1982).

2. *People strive for success in their careers.*
   Individual Psychology further asserts that, since we depend upon the labor of others, work becomes an essential component of life. Therefore, given that humans are constantly striving (Assumption 1), they strive for success in their work life as well as in other areas of their life.

3. *Women who have been publicly recognized for their contributions have achieved a significant degree of success.*
   Since recognition is a major factor in success, and since the assumption is made that all people want to succeed, then public recognition can be considered an indication of success for career women.

4. *Women who are nominated for awards or recognition are successful.*
   The definitions of success in the literature include, in addition to other criteria, recognition and reward by others. Not all

women who are nominated for awards will receive them. Nevertheless, the fact of being nominated is a form of recognition in itself.

5. *Studying successful career women across career fields and levels produces results that can be applied to successful career women in general.* The literature indicates that some common characteristics are shared by career women in general. These include being hard workers, having determination and perseverance, and being committed to their careers.

While specific definitions may apply to career women in given career fields, recognition can be a definition that includes a variety of women in a variety of career fields. This perspective provides information about a wider range of successful career women than has been available.

Chapter 2

Review of Related
Literature

"The rise in the number of working women is probably the single most important change that has ever taken place in the American labor market" (Bloom 1986, 25). There were about 200 percent more working women in 1986 than there were at the end of World War II, according to Bloom. Labor market information suggests that this trend shows no sign of decreasing (see Chapter 1).

This increase has resulted in a variety of research about women and their work. The literature illustrates the complexity of issues that career women face, ranging from child care to style of management to nontraditional careers. A great deal of the research evaluates the career women according to the male model of management, success, or career development. Most of the research focuses on one specific issue (such as management style), targets one portion of the career population (such as executives, managers, or physicians), or compares career women with homemakers or college women.

The review of related literature for this study focuses on the following areas:

1. career development theories
2. career development of women
3. definitions of success

4. characteristics of successful career women
5. achievement/motivation
6. birth order
7. self-esteem

CAREER DEVELOPMENT THEORIES

The trait-factor career theory is the oldest approach to career development theory (Osipow 1983; Zunker 1986). Some of the original theorists include Parsons (1909), Hull (1928), Kitson (1925), and Williamson (1939), although Frank Parsons is generally considered the originator (Zunker 1986).

This theory assumes that (1) people are different in their abilities, (2) individual differences can be measured, (3) different jobs require different skills, and (4) those skills can be measured. Therefore, career development means identifying the best match between the individual's skills and the occupational demands. The approach of the *trait-factor theory* is thus to measure the individual psychometrically, survey occupations to identify needs, and finally match the individual with an occupation. This theory evolved from studies of individual differences in the psychometric movement (Osipow 1973).

The advent of World War I provided an accessible population for the continued development of the trait-factor theory. Psychologists in the U.S. Army needed to classify large numbers of men and assign them to appropriate military jobs. In postwar applications, these data were transposed to civilian occupational groups, as they had been seen in the army. The data served as national norms in vocational guidance and personnel selection (Super 1983).

Ginzberg (1951) and his associates, Ginsburg, Axelrad, and Herma, are generally considered to be the first to approach the theory of occupational choice from a developmental standpoint (Zunker 1981). In developing their theory, they used a carefully selected sample of individuals who would have reasonable freedom in choosing an occupation.

Their sample was comprised of males from middle-upper-class, urban, Protestant or Catholic families of Anglo-Saxon origin, whose educational level ranged from sixth grade to graduate school. Specifically, female and ethnic minority career developmental patterns were not considered. Nor were the rural or urban poor. (Zunker 1983, 5)

Based on this research, Ginzberg concludes that occupational choice is a developmental process. This process generally covers a period of six to ten years and will be completed by approximately age 18 or young adulthood. While the Ginzberg group recognize individual variations in this process, "Individual patterns of career development that lacked conformity with agemates were identified as deviant" (Zunker 1986, 20).

In 1966, Ginzberg wrote that a man achieves his status almost exclusively through his work, while a married woman attains her status largely through her husband. "Until the reemergence of the women's movement in the early 1970s, a woman's success was linked to the significant male in her life, generally her father or husband" (Wood and Greenfeld 1978, 2).

Another early career development theorist was Anne Roe (1957), who focuses on early relationships within the family and their subsequent effects upon the career direction of individuals. She was the first to focus on the personality traits of individuals as a component of career choice.

The analysis of differences in personalities, aptitude, intelligence, and background as related to career choice was the main thrust of her research. She studied several outstanding (male) physical, biological, and social scientists to determine if vocational direction were highly related to early personality development. (Zunker 1983, 7)

Roe wrote "a landmark book on the abilities, interests, and personalities of men and women in various occupational fields (*The Psychology of Occupations,* 1956)" (Super in Walsh and Osipow 1983, 15). She emphasizes that early childhood experiences are primary factors in finding satisfaction in one's chosen field. Super criticizes Roe's assumptions, however, and maintains that she "treated development almost as though it stopped at or soon after entry into school." (p. 16). Super maintains that vocational choices and behaviors can be better understood by "viewing them within the context of the changing demands of the life cycle on the shape of attempts to implement a self-concept." (Osipow 1983, 153).

Roe's theory has three major components. They include (1) the concept of psychic energy, which presumes that each individual has an innate predisposition toward a given level of expending energy; (2) the theory of "need" (specifically Maslow's), which is affected by the type of child-rearing practices of the parents as a major determinant of need fulfillment; and (3) the individual's genetic makeup, which defines their abilities. It should be noted that Maslow's need hierarchy is arranged from lower order, such as food and drink, to higher order, such as love, affection, and self-actualization. The assumption is that the more basic needs (lower order) must be met before the higher order needs (self-actualization) can be addressed (Maslow 1954).

According to Osipow, Roe theorizes that an individual's genetic factors combined with his/her need hierarchy to influence the selection of a vocation. Additionally, the individual's degree of motivation is a product of the intensity and arrangement of each person's need structure. These interactions produce three specific propositions relating to the needs of an individual. First, needs that are regularly satisfied do not contribute to unconscious motivation. Second, higher-order needs, in Maslow's terms, will disappear entirely if they are only rarely satisfied, while the lower-order needs will become dominant motivators if they are only rarely satisfied. Third, when needs are satisfied after an unusual delay, they will, under certain circumstances, become unconscious motivators (Osipow 1983).

It is this portion of Roe's theory that makes it distinctive from other vocational choice theories and from other personality theories. This interactive component emphasizes the importance that child-rearing practices have for vocational choice.

Roe classifies all occupations into two major categories: person-oriented and non-person-oriented (Zunker 1981). She suggests that the individual's early relationships, which are based on the dominant attitude of parental figures, affect the development of personality and therefore the occupational choice of that individual. Roe also explains the different levels of achievement within each occupational group by postulating that there is a given level of psychic energy with which each individual is born. According to Super (1983), Roe's theory can be viewed as a theory of transition from differential vocational psychology to developmental vocational psychology.

In 1951, Donald Super designed a study to follow the vocational development of ninth-grade boys in Middletown, New York (Zunker 1986): "Those individuals who were seen as vocationally mature in the ninth grade (based on their knowledge of occupations, planning, and interests) were significantly more successful as young adults (p. 25). Thus began Super's work on the developmental self-concept theory of career and vocational development (Osipow 1973).

Super postulates that self-concept development is a result of a combination of factors that include genetic, psychological, and environmental variables. He further contends that self-concept development is open to outside intervention and is most malleable during early adolescence. This age, therefore, will be the most appropriate time for career development information and intervention (Osipow 1973).

In developing his theory of vocational behavior, Super proposed a sequence of five vocational developmental stages and five vocational developmental tasks (Fredrickson 1982; Osipow 1973; Super et al. 1963; and Zunker 1986). He identifies the stages and links them with approximate ages. The first, stage 1 (Growth—birth to age 14 or 15), incorporates the development of interests, attitudes, capacities, and needs that are associated with self-concept. Stage 2 (Exploratory—ages 15 to 24) is a time of narrowing choices, transition, trials, and tentative decisions. Stage 3 (Establishment—ages 25 to 44) is also a time for transition, but leads into stabilization. Stage 4 (Maintenance—ages 45 to 64) incorporates the adjustment to the working situation and is composed of consistent work in a given field. Stage 5 (Decline—age 65 +) consists of pre-retirement considerations.

These stages provide the framework for the vocational behavior and attitudes incorporated in the corresponding vocational development tasks. Task 1 (Crystallization—approximately ages 14 to 18) is the cognitive process period, when the individual formulates a general vocational goal based on his or her awareness of resources, as well as on interests and values. Task 2 (Specification—ages 18 to 21) occurs when the individual moves from a tentative vocational preference to a more specific one. The completion of this task requires formalizing and clarifying one's decision. Task 3 (Implementation—ages 21 to 24) involves the completion of training and entry into actual employment.

Task 4 (Stabilization—ages 24 to 35) occurs through confirming a preferred career by actual work experience and the use of talents that demonstrate the appropriateness of the individual's career choice. Finally, Task 5 (Consolidation—age 35+) results in the individual's establishment in a career, focusing on advancement, status, and seniority.

Super (1960) believes that the completion of the appropriate task at each level of development indicates "vocational maturity." This vocational maturity leads to a stable or conventional career pattern. He later (1976) postulated that individuals are capable of moving through these stages and tasks at differing paces, as well as returning to earlier stages when appropriate. The formulation of this concept softens the earlier, more static pattern of development (Osipow 1973).

Super also categorizes both male and female career patterns in a 1957 essay (in Zunker 1986). He identifies four career patterns for males:

1. *Stable,* defined as early entry into a career with little or no trial work period.

2. *Conventional,* characterized by trial work periods followed by entry into a stable pattern.

3. *Unstable,* defined as a series of trial jobs.

4. *Multiple-trial,* or the non-establishment of a career as signified by continual change of employment.

For females, he classified career patterns into seven categories:

1. *Stable homemaking,* defined as marriage before any significant work experience.

2. *Conventional career,* defined as entry into work after high school or college as a stop-gap, which is then followed by marriage and full-time homemaking.

3. *Stable working career,* defined as entry into work following training; viewed as a lifetime career.

4. *Double-track career,* defined as entry into a career after training, then marriage and the second career of homemaking.

5. *Interrupted career*, defined as entry into work, followed by marriage and the dropping of the career for full-time home-making. The woman may return to the career depending upon the circumstances in the home.

6. *Unstable*, defined as a cyclical pattern of working, dropping out of work to resume full-time homemaking, only to repeat the pattern again.

7. *Multiple-trial career*, defined as the non-establishment of a career, marked by continual change of employment.

In five out of the seven categories, the career patterns for women emphasize that women are expected to pursue the role of wife and homemaker. This expectation is a factor regardless of whatever else they may choose (Zunker 1981).

Career development theories are constantly being researched and introduced for consideration. More recent career theorists, such as John Holland, David Tiedeman, John Crites, and Robert O'Hara, have contributed significantly to the field of career development theory.

John Holland began the development of his theory while working with the American College Testing program in a post–World War II veterans hospital (Walsh and Osipow 1983). He modified his original theoretical statement (1959) as a result of research testing the theory. He postulates that career choices represent an extension of one's personality and that occupational choice is a process of matching oneself with a given situation.

He groups fields of work into six major categories called modal personality types. The six categories are realistic, investigative, artistic, social, enterprising, and conventional. He "used the same six homogeneous categories to classify occupations as he does for personality orientations" (Fredrickson 1982, 29). These categories are based on the nature of the work involved and the adjectives used by judges to describe the individuals doing the work. Holland proposes that individuals are a composite of personality types, with a preferential ordering or dominant orientation that defines their personal modal orientation. While his theory does not explicitly discuss the manner in which the modal orientations develop (Osipow 1973), it does identify the manner in which the modal orientations influence career choice and vocational behavior.

In addition to this modal orientation, Holland believes that individuals choose their level within the occupation hierarchy as a function of their intelligence and degree of self-knowledge and self-evaluation. The congruence of individuals' "view of self" with their occupational preference is what Holland refers to as the modal personal style (Zunker 1986, 28).

According to Osipow (1983), Holland introduced the concept of self-knowledge, which is defined as "the amount and accuracy of information an individual has about him or herself" (p. 87). Holland maintains that the adequacy of the occupational choice relates directly to the adequacy of the self-knowledge and occupational knowledge of an individual. The *environment* is thus considered to be a significant shaper of the development of personal choice (Osipow 1983, 89).

Tiedeman and O'Hara formulate their career decision theory based on the concepts of Ginzberg and associates (Osipow 1983). Their more complex, graphic, "and thus a more realistic system . . . stresses the role of self concept in negotiating developmental stages and includes a complicated and sophisticated set of developmental notions" (Osipow 1983, 207). They suggest, however, that the decision-making process does not begin until the individual recognizes that a vocational problem exists.

Career development, according to Tiedeman and O'Hara (Zunker 1986), takes place within the individual's general process of cognitive development as he or she moves through the eight life stages, or "psychosocial crises" (Zunker 1986, 32) as defined by Erikson (1950). The eight psychosocial crises are: (1) trust, (2) autonomy, (3) initiative, (4) industry, (5) identity, (6) intimacy, (7) generativity, and (8) ego integrity. Tiedeman "believes the evolving ego identity is of central importance in the career development process" (Zunker 1986, 31).

Based on Erikson's stages as a foundation, they postulate that an interaction takes place between the development of an individual's decision-making ability and the development of the individual's ego and values. They group the stages of career decision-making into two categories: (1) anticipation and (2) implementation and adjustment. These categories include seven stages that parallel Erikson's life stages. The stages are: (1) exploration, (2) crystallization, (3) choice, (4) clarification or specification, (5) induction, (6) transition or reformation, and (7) integration or maintenance (Tiedeman and O'Hara 1963; Fredrickson 1982; Osipow 1983; Zunker 1986). These stages fall into the following two categories accordingly. The first category is the period of anticipation or preoccupation. It includes these stages:

1. exploration
2. crystallization
3. choice
4. clarification or specification

The second category is the period of implementation and adjustment. It includes the stages of:

1. induction
2. transition or reformation
3. maintenance or integration

   Each of these seven stages includes specific characteristics. The exploration stage consists of thinking that is transitory in nature; considering several possible courses of action; imagining oneself in various situations; searching and projecting into tentative goals; envisioning future behavior with alternative courses of action; and reflecting on aspirations, abilities, and interests with consideration of the societal implications related to career choice. The crystallization stage includes the continued assessment of alternatives and narrowing the possible alternatives, which leads to the emergence of tentative choices and then the rank ordering of those choices. Goals become more clarified and definite but are not locked in; there is a definite move toward stability of thought. The choice stage is reached when a definite goal is chosen and the individual focuses on the behavior required to reach the identified goal. The clarification or specification stage marks the end of the anticipation category. It is when further consideration of the career lessens the doubts about the decision and when a stronger conviction about the career decision develops.

The second category of implementation and adjustment begins with the stage of induction. This stage is characterized by the beginning of the social interaction experience as the individual begins career identification; continued identification and definition of the self within the career social system; the experience of acceptance within the career; and the further progress of the individual's goal within the framework of the career. The second stage of this category, reformation or transition, includes the acknowledgement and acceptance by the career group; assertive action on the part of the individual within the career group to convince others of the new self-view held by the individual; and movement toward greater acceptance of modified goals. The final stage of maintenance or integration is characterized by compromise or realignment of goals as the individual interacts with the career group; the attainment of objectivity about oneself and the career group; emergence of the identification of the working member within the career field; and satisfaction when a committed cause or action is attained, at least temporarily. (Fredrickson 1982; Zunker 1986).

These stages identify crucial decision points for the individual, although they have no rigidly set time frame. The duration and timing of these developmental stages, however, are of prime importance to the career development of the individual. Tiedeman maintains that the duration and timing of the developmental stages is affected by individual biological requirements (such as the amount of sleep required), as well as by personal characteristics (such as role identification). Therefore, these stages are time flexible but "fit within the overall pattern of human development" (Zunker 1986, 35).

Like Super and Ginzberg, Tiedeman and O'Hara "see these decisions taking place over a lifetime in which the individual seeks both to differentiate him or herself from others and also how to integrate themselves into a productive part of society" (Fredrickson 1982, 34). They maintain that society and the individual tend to work continually toward a common goal— that is, to identify and establish what meaning each has for the other (Tiedeman and O'Hara 1963; Zunker 1986).

Tiedeman has, with others (Miller-Tiedeman and Niemi 1977; Dudley and Tiedeman 1977; Peatling and Tiedeman 1977;

Miller-Tiedeman and Tiedeman 1982; Tiedeman and Miller-Tiedeman 1977, 1984), further developed his earlier conceptualizations of the career decision-making process. The more recent focus emphasizes individuals' taking more control of the decision-making process by comprehending more about themselves. This action provides the individual with "I-power," which is defined as the potential for self improvement (Fredrickson 1982; Zunker 1986). Individuals must master eight skills before obtaining I-power, according to Miller-Tiedeman and Niemi (1977). They are:

1. Becoming more conscious of themselves, in order to cooperate with momentary and daily evolutions;
2. Living more frequently in the now, rather than in the future and past;
3. Becoming more planful and acting on their plans;
4. Waking up to making their lives happen, rather than just sleeping and letting their lives happen;
5. Trusting themselves, in order to tolerate anxiety when facing uncertainty;
6. Being sensitive to others as they gain I-power—not power over but power with and among other people;
7. Recognizing and discarding old ways of thinking through self-remembering;
8. Being honest with themselves. (Miller-Tiedeman and Niemi 1977, 5)

Tiedeman and O'Hara view career development as a process occurring within identified time stages. This operation is seen as a continuously operating, systematic problem-solving procedure that focuses on increased self-awareness as a vital component of the career decision-making process. According to Zunker, this focus on self-awareness is a major contribution to the field of career development theory. However, he states that:

While this theory has had an important impact on the career-decision process, it is limited by lack of empirical data. It was theoretically formulated in accord with Erikson's stages on the basis of the vocationally relevant experiences of five white males. (Zunker 1986, 35)

John Krumboltz, a social learning theorist, among others (Osipow 1983), has designed a theory of career decision making. It defines how career interests develop, the effect of the environment on an individual's career decision making, and how career decision-making skills are developed. The career decision-making theory is based on the social learning theory as proposed by Bandura (1969) and emphasizes a clear specification of treatment and outcome (Fredrickson 1982).

As with other career development theories, the social learning theory of career development attempts to identify and explain the personal and environmental events that shape an individual's decisions about careers. Krumboltz maintains that the career decision-making process is influenced by four factors: (1) genetic endowment, (2) environmental conditions and events, (3) learning experiences, and (4) task approach skills (Osipow 1983; Zunker 1986). Genetic endowment includes inherited attributes, such as gender and physical appearance along with "apparently inherited abilities involving motor, intellective, and perceptual behaviors" (Osipow 1983, 144). The environmental conditions and events include the individual's experiences in the job market, social policies, available role models, and training options. Factors ranging from family resources to technological developments and from global events such as war and natural disasters to educational opportunities and achievements also play a part (Fredrickson 1982).

Krumboltz et al. (1976) propose that the career learning experiences occur within the three main categories of social learning theory. These three categories are: (1) reinforcement, whereby certain behaviors, attitudes, and decisions are rewarded by the environment or the self; (2) modeling, which entails observing another person, of some perceived status, engaging in certain behaviors and then seeing that person rewarded and/or punished for those behaviors; and (3) contiguous pairing or classical conditioning, whereby certain behaviors or attitudes coincide with a reward or a punishment, so that the behavior is subsequently approached or avoided, even when the original reward or punishment is no longer present (Bandura 1969).

All of these forms of learning affect the individual and play a major part in the development of their task approach skills. Through the learning experiences, the individual learns to apply a range of attitudes and skills involving work habits, values, problem-solving skills, emotional responses, and cognitive skills related to new tasks. These skills help the individual engage in the career decision-making process and ultimately lead to the solution of their career-related problems. Therefore, the individual's readiness for decision making is equated with career maturity (Osipow 1983; Zunker 1986; Krumboltz et al. 1976).

The social learning theorists maintain that since interests are a result of the learning process, learning leads people to make career choices (Krumboltz 1973, 1976). Consequently, career development is seen as a process in which a change in learning can produce a change in interests and preferences, and thereby a change in career decisions. This model posits a lifelong process involving a learned skill and emphasizes the importance of learning experiences (Fredrickson 1982; Krumboltz 1976; Osipow 1983; Zunker 1986).

Summary of Career Development Theories

These career development theorists illustrate the direction of career development since the field was defined in Parson's work in 1909. Particularly among most early theorists, the population used in studying career development and establishing the norms for career tests, interest inventories, and so forth was most often white, Anglo-Saxon males.

As Osipow (1973) has noted, the theories of career development have, since their beginning, focused on the male population. Later theories continued to select males for study, but with more emphasis on personality factors. The career decision-making theory of Tiedeman and O'Hara and Krumboltz's social learning theory come closer to avoiding gender bias with their focus on environmental and developmental factors. Even so, the foundations were laid for career development theory based on male standards.

CAREER DEVELOPMENT OF WOMEN

The research and career development theories continued to focus on the male population until the 1960s when, due to the changing roles of women and their increasing presence in the work force, scholars began to challenge some long-held assumptions about women and work. These common assumptions include that (1) the primary roles of women are those of wife and mother, and their work revolves around household/domestic and childcare responsibilities; (2) women who do work do so only because of an unfortunate need and, because of this "unfortunate need," their career goals/needs must be different; and (3) any male career development theory can be generalized to explain women's career development (Fitzgerald and Betz, 1983).

Fitzgerald and Betz challenge the first assumption of "women's place" being exclusively in the home. They maintain that women working outside the home in ever-increasing numbers are a vital part of the labor force. They state that "Women whose adult lives will not include work outside the home are increasingly becoming the exception rather than the norm" (1983, 84).

Second, Fitzgerald and Betz's review of research indicates that the majority of young women prefer to combine marriage and career pursuits in their adult lives. The assumption that women's career development can be described or predicted using existing theories also is untenable, according to Fitzgerald and Betz, because of several clearly evident sex differences relevant to vocational choices and patterns. These differences include that (1) women tend to be concentrated in a small number of "traditionally female" jobs and professions; (2) career aspirations of young women continue to focus on stereotypically female occupations; (3) the socialization of women to pursue the same (traditionally female) roles, regardless of their individual capabilities and talents; and (4) women's career development involves one more step than men must make. Women must decide if employment will be a major focus in their life, and if so, whether they choose to juggle the roles of worker/spouse/parent. At least some thought must be given to how children and/or career can be ordered, given the biological limitations of childbearing time for women and the inherent or covert limitations of some careers. Men are not subject to this series of choices or decisions, for they are not given the option of whether or not to work—only what work they would like to pursue. "Men in this society grow up assuming that they will need to support themselves and their families, and, thus, begin with the choice of an occupation rather than with the choice of whether or not to work" (Fitzgerald and Betz 1983, 87).

Issues concerning equality, political rights, professional opportunities, and economics evolved from the feminist movement in the early 1970s. "Women and some men are today trying to find viable, productive, satisfying alternatives to the stifling sexual stereotypes of the past" (Low 1973, 98). In an issue of *School Review* devoted to women and education, Kagan uses the term "masculine narcissism" to refer to the prevailing historical assumptions that contribute to restrictive stereotypes about the limited intelligence of women. He concludes a section of his article on left hemispheric advantage by stating:

Perhaps it is woman, not man, who is the intellectual specialist; woman, not man, who insists on interlacing sensory experience with meaning. These reversals of popular homilies join other maxims that science has begun to question. For now we know that it is the female, not the male, who is most predictable; the female, not the male, who is biologically more resistant to infirmity; the female's anatomy, not the male's, that is nature's preferred form. Man's a priori guesses about sex differences have reflected an understandable but excessive masculine narcissism. (Kagan 1972, 223)

Referring to Kagan's 1972 hypothesis, Howe states that " 'masculine narcissism' dominates our culture, controlling our language as well as our major institutions. Most completely, such bias controls the futures of young females and males" (1973, 109).

As recently as 1970, the New York Academy of Sciences sponsored a workshop called "The Impact of Fertility Limitation on Women's Life-Career and Personality" (Kundsin 1973). In this workshop, many of the previously held assumptions on sex roles were questioned, in particular the stereotype of the female sex role, which, while historically comfortable because it requires no choice for women, is emotionally laden and currently obsolete. Confining women to this traditional role is not good either for the individual or for society. It is "philosophically no longer acceptable from a humanistic and ethical standpoint" (Low 1973, 98).

In 1984, Helen Astin proposed a beginning formulation of a new model of career development. She asserts that it "can be used to explain the occupational behavior of both genders" (Astin 1984, 118). She labels it a "sociopsychological" model because it includes both personal characteristics and social forces, and it shows how these two variables interact. This developmental model contains four major constructs: motivation, expectations, sex-role socialization, and the structure of opportunity (Astin 1984).

Astin draws on Roe's career development theory and Bandura's social learning theory to demonstrate how women's occupational expectations are shaped by their socialization experiences. She states: "My premise is that basic work motivation is the same for men and women, but that they make different choices because their early socialization experiences and structural opportunities are different" (Astin 1984, 118).

In reviewing Astin's theory, Gilbert (1984) and Fitzgerald and Betz (1984) question some of her assumptions. Gilbert comments that "active participation in family roles is assumed to be harmonious with occupational achievement and advancement." The article continues: "Can a concept of career that includes involvement in family and occupational roles (and principles of equity between men and women) realistically co-exist with social institutions that embody the values of a patriarchal society?" (Gilbert 1984, 129). Fitzgerald and Betz note that "although Astin should be congratulated for her insistence on the importance of social forces in shaping behavior, she fails to give credit where credit is due; to the most influential social force of this century: the women's movement" (1984, 137).

It is important to note *how* men and women are viewed differently in the literature. Here are four specific examples of this difference in views. First, during the preschool years, girls and boys are treated more nearly as equals than they ever will be treated again. Although females are told from the first grade on that they are equal with men, they are treated in a manner that negates the statement (Ampola 1973). The sometimes overt, often covert, attitudes and practices in public education reinforce the inequality between male and female. Schools emphasize the inferiority of the female, as exemplified by the lack of expectation for female math ability or physical strength (Howe 1973).

Second, the societal expectations for males and females can be identified by how the research questions are asked. An example is Ralph Turner's 1964 research, cited in Wood and Greenfeld (1978, 4), in which he studied high school seniors in Los Angeles. Turner's index for male ambition includes three factors: expected occupation in 20 years, desire for material wealth, and expected educational attainment. His index for female ambition includes only two factors: the minimum occupation they would expect their husbands to occupy in 20 years and their material expectations. Turner concludes that "the husband's occupation is the key status for most women in American society" (Turner 1964, 2).

Third, the stereotypes in children's readers and textbooks limit the perspectives of girls and women. Brothers lead relatively active lives and perform before their sisters, who, not surprisingly, admire male agility and inventiveness. "Girls are prepared in all these books to be fumblers at physical activities, to function as listeners, watchers, waiters, rather than doers. Most of all, girls are prepared to be mothers, and mothers in school texts are invariably docile" (Howe 1973, 111).

Fourth, the fact that others have different expectations for each gender influences the manner in which boys and girls view themselves and each other. If we aim at blurring all distinctions between the sexes, it might result in the destruction of certain biases against women. Alternatively, students might study stereotypes in order to decide for themselves about patterns for the future. "I believe that it is foolish to deny their [differences] existence—among individuals or between classes, races, sexes, groups of any sort. I believe that we may learn from the study of differences as much as we learn from similarities" (Howe 1973, 113).

Career Development of Women Summary

The focus of career development theory and research began to shift from male-only subjects to the inclusion of females in the 1960s, due to the significantly increasing numbers of women in the work force. Long-held assumptions about women and work were challenged. This change included challenging assumptions about why women work. Current research cites the personal desire for careers as well as increased economic necessity as reasons for women to work outside the home. The assumption that career development theory could be transferred from males to females was challenged by recognizing that career choices of men and women are affected in part by societal expectations based on gender. As a result, career development and career choice are also affected by gender. Women must decide if they will juggle the roles of career/spouse/parent, and if so, must give some thought to how that combination could possibly be structured. Choosing to combine roles sometimes results in restrictions of career choice, due to the covert limitations of some careers.

DEFINITIONS OF SUCCESS

Definitions of success, for individuals and for careers, vary widely among those doing the defining. The following definitions of success will include those offered by personality theory, by the dictionary, and by researchers.

The personality theory of Alfred Adler (1870-1937), termed Individual Psychology (Manaster and Corsini 1982), includes several assumptions about what constitutes success for human beings, as well as about the relationship of individuals to work (careers). Individual Psychology maintains that "All behavior occurs in a social context" (Mosak and Dreikurs 1973, 39), that the feeling of belonging and of being a part of the larger social whole (of contributing to society) is a basic desire of humans. Individual Psychology "sees individuals constantly in the process of striving" (Manaster and Corsini 1982, 5), with individuals consistently moving toward self-selected goals.

"Individual Psychology firmly takes the position that we are indivisible units" (Manaster and Corsini 1982, 2). As individuals, not just an assemblage of parts, we must be understood as a unity, and each unity has its own subjective reality. According to Manaster and Corsini:

Two people may have exactly the same goals, the same amount of energy, everything may appear identical, but one has courage and pursues goals actively, persistently, intelligently, and consistently, while another person will hesitate, fumble, and back away. For this reason, directed activity—going after one's goals in a sensible manner—is a prerequisite of a successful life. (p. 11)

According to Adler, personal success is a function of an individual's social interest. This social interest includes an "identification with humanity, a feeling of community, or belonging to life" (Manaster and Corsini 1982, 13).

Another assumption of Individual Psychology is that "Life presents challenges in the form of life tasks" (Mosak and Dreikurs 1973, 41). One of the life tasks is work. They state that "Each of us is dependent upon the labor of other people. In turn, they are dependent upon our contribution. Work thus becomes essential for human survival. The cooperative individual assumes this role willingly" (p. 42).

Adlerian assumptions about successful human beings include that: (1) all behavior occurs in a social context; (2) belonging (being part of the larger social whole) is a central striving of all individuals; (3) each unity has its own subjective reality; (4) humans are constantly striving toward self-selected goals; (5) success in life is related to the individual's degree of social interest; and (6) work is a life task in which cooperative individuals participate willingly.

According to Webster's dictionary (1975), success is a favorable termination of a venture, the attainment of wealth, favor, or eminence. Success, simply defined then, relates to the achievement of goals, and, according to Adlerian psychology, goals vary with individuals. In the literature, there are almost as many definitions of success as there are books or research articles on successful career women.

Blotnick's work contributes to the literature on researchers' definitions of career success. In reporting on his 25-year study of who does well in the workplace, Blotnick states that "Social beings that humans are, they want their labors to be recognized and rewarded by others. . . . When all is said and done, what matters most is that recognition in some form is finally theirs" (Blotnick 1985, 3).

Some of the more frequently used criteria for successful career women include: having management positions, particularly in the corporate world; being in top administrative posts; working in male-dominated fields; receiving high salaries (Trahey 1977); being recognized by experts in their field; attaining positions of status and power (such as chief executive officer); and supervising others (Keown and Keown 1985).

In their study of successful women in business, the Keowns identify successful women as those who work for profit-making organizations, who manage subordinates in an executive position, and who earn a minimum of $25,000 annually (Keown and Keown 1985). Trahey (1977) equates success with high salaries (over $50,000) and power, particularly in the corporate world.

Kundsin identifies successful women as those "who have made it up the ladder in male-oriented fields and are so identified by their peers" (1973, 99). She proposes that many more women could be called successful if the definition of success were more open-ended and included those who have an inner sense of their own identity, worth, and self-esteem as a person, without reference to career accomplishments or money.

Wood and Greenfeld compare the meaning of success for career women in male- and female-dominated occupations. They find that while women across occupations rank the listed definitions of success similarly, the intensity of the responses vary between women in male- and female-dominated jobs. "Women in male-dominated jobs indicated a higher need to define success as 'recognition from others on the job,' 'becoming an authority,' 'achieving a high salary,' and 'obtaining a title of responsibility' " (1978,24). In contrast, "being well-liked" is the first choice for women in female-dominated jobs (p. 17).

Investigating women of distinction in psychology, science, the arts, and politics, Bachtold (1976) uses attainment of a doctoral degree and affiliation with a college or university as criteria of success. By contrast, Waddell (1982), in his study on the self-employed female, states that: "owners' success was measured by the length of time in business. It was assumed that more successful owners would be able to remain in business longer than the less successful owners" (p. 299).

In their study of successful, high-achieving women in atypical professions (medicine and law), Williams and McCullers establish four levels of success. "The four categories within each field ranged from very atypical (the high success category) to very traditional occupations for females" (1983, 346). The categories in medicine are:

1. highly successful physician,
2. practicing physician,
3. licensed practical nurse (LPN), and
4. certified medical assistant or administrative personnel.

In law the categories are:

1. highly successful lawyer,
2. practicing lawyer,
3. certified court reporter, and
4. legal secretary.

They designate Category 1, the very atypical, as highly successful. The subjects were selected for inclusion in this category by a panel of three experts in each field. The criterion used is nomination by at least two of the three experts.

Successful women administrators in the educational field are identified by Temmen (1982) as either full-time project directors in educational laboratories, one of the top 10 to 20 administrators at the central administration office, or a building administrator or principal with stature equal to the central office administrators named.

In their well-known study of women managers, Hennig and Jardim (1977) identify a successful woman manager in part as:

one who has had a full-time, continuous work history, holds a current position at the level of corporate vice president or president or chief

executive officer of a corporation or large divisional operation . . . a
position which appears to represent line authority and would probably
include the management of men . . . and . . . not employed in a position
or type of business generally considered as "feminine" (for example
retailing or the cosmetics industry). (p. 66)

Halcomb (1979) implies that winning power, fame, and money
(based on male patterns of success) and being at or near the top
of their field or organization identify successful career women.
Others, such as Abi-Karam and Love and Pinkstaff and Wilkinson (1979), hold a more nebulous definition of success. They
identify it as a recognized measure of achievement (Abi-Karam
and Love 1984, 2) or as living up to one's own goals, desires, and
expectations (Pinkstaff and Wilkinson 1979, 84).

What about women in all levels of careers? To assume that a
woman who is not "in management" or "earning $50,000" or in
an "atypical" profession is therefore unsuccessful denies the
value of a multitude of female-dominated careers. How do the
women in typical and atypical career fields define success? What
do they have in common?

Summary of Definitions of Success

The definitions of success include the degree of social interest
expressed by an individual and the striving toward self-selected
goals, as identified by Adlerian psychology; recognition and
reward by others; and the attainment of wealth, favor, or eminence. Definitions specifically for career women range from having management positions in the corporate world to the attainment of a doctoral degree to receiving a salary of over $50,000.

One of the common themes in much of the literature concerns
visibility or recognition as a measure of the successful career
woman. In many cases, subjects are solicited for study by asking
experts in the field and/or top management to identify the most
successful women in a given group. Although specific definitions
of success may be valid for specific populations of women in
given career fields, a more encompassing definition of success—recognition by others—must be used in order to include a
variety of women in a variety of careers.

If the assumptions are made that everyone wants to succeed
and that recognition is one factor of success, then success via

recognition can be a common denominator for studying career women. Using this criterion allows for a wider range of occupations to be investigated at one time and places fewer limitations on the population of career women.

CHARACTERISTICS OF SUCCESSFUL
CAREER WOMEN

In their study of successful managerial women, Hennig and Jardim (1977) identify some characteristics that these women have in common. These include having some idea of their future career goals; achieving these goals through their own efforts; lacking the effort (or awareness of the need) to promote their own visibility within the organization with the people who mattered; and achieving position and status in spite of many barriers. These women tend to be pioneers, "not simply in terms of their unusual accomplishments but in the difficulties they overcame and the price they paid to break open new territory" (p. 65).

The personality needs profile developed by Abi-Karam and Love (1984) suggests that the achieving woman has a unique personality profile. This profile reflects "leaders with a strong ability to influence their environment. They are motivated to do their best, to be a recognized authority, and to accomplish significantly in a 'man's world' " (p. 6). Further, they tend to be independent, unconventional, and nonconforming. "Their self-esteem is based more upon self-evaluation than on the opinion of others" (p. 7). Abi-Karam and Love go on to suggest that achieving women redefine for themselves an expanded concept of femininity to include masculine instrumental behaviors.

Keown and Keown (1982) suggest that for the corporate woman executive to be successful, she must have a strong commitment to a career; postpone or minimize the number of children she has; maintain a positive attitude toward self and work; stay within jobs concerned with people, information, and money; and, finally, realize that job competence or expertise is crucial for women executives.

In a later study, the Keowns (1985) find that most of these executive women seem "to be able to integrate marriage into their lives and still give their career goals a high priority" (p. 281).

The personal characteristics for success, identified by the subjects, include: hard work and determination; the ability to interact well with people; the ability to communicate and to do the job well; an enjoyment of their work; a desire for accomplishment; and a willingness to be measured.

In her study of successful women in nursing who have earned doctoral degrees, Zimmerman (1983) identifies six personal characteristics that are both rated and ranked highly by the women. These qualities are responsibility, perseverance, hard work commitment to a career, being person-oriented, and competence on the job. Additionally, these women rank their personal characteristics as the most important factor facilitating their career success.

Feulner (1979) considers professional women who are lawyers, physicians, or professors and finds that they

are a singular group of women, who seem to be more influenced by the demands of professional life than by the societal definition of "proper" feminine attitudes and behavior. They tend to be somewhat more aggressive, dominant, autonomous, and self-confident than "average" women. (p. 68)

She goes on to suggest that these women professionals enjoy their uniqueness and have no guilt about being "different." While they are aware that being a woman is sometimes a handicap in professional life, there is no resentment about their gender.

Halcomb (1979) conducted interviews with successful career women of vastly different career fields, backgrounds, and interests. She describes these women as generally enthusiastic, committed, dedicated, energetic, efficient, and "being very good at not wasting time" (p. 163). The women interviewed mention such personal characteristics as being able to concentrate on the matter at hand; doing each job well; being decisive; taking responsibility for decisions; taking risks and being willing to make a mistake; promoting their own visibility; and not taking everything personally (being task-oriented rather than ego-oriented).

Blotnick (1985) notes that "Women who went on to become successful at work and at home never became addicted to outrage" (p. 224). These successful women use their daily supply of energy efficiently, apply continuous mental effort to the tasks at hand, work hard, have moderate (rather than unrealistically high) expectations, and do not set rigid career goals. They tend to have general goals, rather than rigidly specific ones. "We found that the vast majority of men and women who succeed do so in a way that few of them forecast" (p. 239).

Temmen (1982), Nieva and Gutek (1981), and Frieze et al. (1978) conclude that the characteristics of successful career women generally include emotional maturity, independence, competence, realism, courage, ambition, career commitment, self-confidence, and education. Bachtold (1976) identifies qualities that professional women who are psychologists, scientists, artists, and writers, and politicians share, in contrast to women in general. Such women must behave in ways that indicate good mental capacity; not conform with traditional sex-role expectations; have a low reactivity to threat; and be assertive and inclined to experiment with problems.

Summary of Characteristics of Successful Career Women

The literature indicates that successful career women do share some common characteristics. Some of the most frequently mentioned are hard work, determination, perseverance, commitment to their careers, and an idea of the direction they want to pursue, although they generally do not set rigid goals. Furthermore, the women in male-dominated professions have other characteristics in common, such as being more aggressive, independent, self-confident, autonomous, and unconventional.

ACHIEVEMENT/MOTIVATION

Many theorists have contributed to the ongoing study of achievement/motivation. These include Sigmund Freud (1856-1939) with his psychoanalytic theory, Clark Hull (1884-1952) with his mechanistic drive theory, and Kurt Lewin (1890-1947) with his field theory (see Weiner 1985).

The study of achievement/motivation has been strongly influenced by Henry Murray's development of a taxonomy of 20 basic needs (which included achievement) and his development of the thematic apperception test (TAT) in 1938. This test was aimed at assessing need states and, according to Weiner (1985), was almost universally adopted by subsequent investigators for the study of achievement/motivation.

Murray (1938) defines the achievement need as the desire: "To accomplish something difficult. . . . To overcome obstacles and attain a high standard. To excel one's self. To rival and surpass others. To increase self-regard by the successful exercise of talent" (Weiner 1985, 180). He further maintains that these achievement desires are accompanied by the following actions: "To make intense, prolonged and repeated efforts to accomplish something difficult. To work with singleness of purpose towards a high and distant goal . . . to enjoy competition. To try to do everything well. To exert will power; to overcome boredom and fatigue" (Weiner, 180). Frieze et al. (1978) briefly defines achievement as a desire to do things well and be successful. He contends that while women are motivated to succeed, they define success differently than men do.

According to Weiner (1985), theorists McClelland and Atkinson have both contributed greatly to the refinement of the TAT and to subsequent research on achievement/motivation. Their definition means to strive for success in any situation where standards of excellence are applicable. Stein and Bailey (1973) maintain that this concept of achievement/motivation has received relatively good support in studies of males, but not of females. Additionally, they have reviewed Atkinson's 1966 achievement/motivation formulation—that the principal behavioral indicators of aroused motivation are achievement effort and level of aspiration. They conclude that this formulation does not apply to females because, "virtually no research has been conducted with females using this expanded theoretical formulation" (p. 346). Chusmir (1985) agrees that the male-oriented TAT is not appropriate to measure the motivation of women.

Weiner (1985) contends that the most popular theories of achievement/motivation have incorporated the expectancy-value concept. This concept means that the choice among achievement activities and the amount of effort toward achieving those goals are thought to be determined by how an individual values success and his or her own expectancy of success.

Atkinson's early work with achievement/motivation suggests that "achievement behavior was a function of both desire for success . . . and anxiety or fear of failure" (Frieze et al. 1978, 237). This fear is believed to be instrumental in keeping people from achievement activities in which they might fail.

Horner (1972) suggests that in addition to Atkinson's motives to succeed and to avoid failure, a third motive exists for women: the motive to avoid success. This concept has been labeled "fear of success" (Nieva and Gutek 1981, 94). Reviewing the research, Nieva and Gutek challenge the stability of Horner's fear of success in females and suggest that this "so-called motive is a reflection of cultural stereotype" (p. 95). White et al. (1981) identify inconsistent results across studies of fear of success and suggest that more work needs to be done "before valid generalizable conclusions can be made" (p. 559). Weiner (1985) corroborates the challenge to Horner's fear of success theory, stating that "subsequent research has revealed that males exhibit as much fear of success in projective imagery as females. In summary, the findings first reported by Horner are now very much in doubt" (p. 223).

Achievement theory has focused on the role of individual differences in achievement needs in an attempt to understand the motivational processes. Weiner (1985) states that based on the research:

there is suggestive evidence that tasks of intermediate difficulty are more attractive to individuals highly motivated to succeed than to those lower in achievement needs. And individuals high in achievement needs have been characterized as "realistic" and have occupational goals that are congruent with their abilities. (P. 189)

Veroff (cited in Stein and Bailey, 1973) reports that the selection of an intermediate difficulty level indicates a high achievement/motivation, and "the fact that the sexes are about equally likely to choose this adaptive [intermediate] level of aspiration is *important* because boys' higher levels of aspiration have sometimes been interpreted as indicators of greater motivation" (p. 355).

Weiner (1985) summarizes that other characteristics of indi-

viduals high in the need for achievement include: a preference
for personal feedback; better ability to delay gratification than
those low in need for achievement; and higher grades in school,
if grades are instrumental to long-term success. These individuals are conceptualized as "hope" oriented rather than "fear"
oriented. They take personal responsibility for their success,
have high feelings of self-worth, and generally perceive themselves as high in ability.

Studies involving professional women, particularly in law and
medicine (Williams and McCullers 1983 and Abi-Karam and
Love 1984) indicate that these women are more similar to male
norms in achievement needs. Abi-Karam and Love state that
professional women "are motivated to do their best, to be a
recognized authority, and to accomplish significantly in a 'man's
world' " (p. 6). Williams and McCullers also note that professional women, particularly in law, have high scores on the need-
achievement measure. Further, women in both law and medicine
"revealed a consistent picture of strong family support for
achievement efforts, even though these efforts were not always
stereotypically feminine" (p. 354).

Other research on achievement/motivation includes Powers
and Wagner's studies of achievement/motivation in middle and
high school students (1984a, 1984b). Among middle school boys
and girls, the attribution of success to effort is the best predictor
of achievement/motivation. In a study of combined middle and
high school students, achievement/motivation correlates attributions of school success positively with effort and ability. The researchers state: "A higher correlation was found between
achievement motivation and the attributions of success to effort . . . than to ability" (Powers and Wagner 1984b, 220). These
results suggest that attributions of success to internal causes
may result in increased effort and motivation among students.

Achievement/Motivation Summary

Achievement/motivation has been the focus of considerable research, and differences between males and females have been
postulated (Horner 1972). Stein and Bailey (1973) identify a
major problem with achievement/motivation theory, stating:
"Like much psychological theory, achievement/motivation theory

was developed to explain the behavior of males. Then attempts were made to use that theory with females. Not surprisingly, it does not work as well for females" (p. 362).

Other patterns in the research include the lack of focus on ethnic groups other than white middle-class subjects and the lack of achievement/motivation needs defined appropriately for females. Additionally, studies involving achievement/motivation and ordinal position have revealed differences in achievement/ motivation related to gender and ordinal positions (Falbo 1981; Jordan et al. 1982; Snell et al. 1986).

BIRTH ORDER

In considering the development of personality, the Individual Psychology theory of Alfred Adler identifies two very important aspects of human behavior. Manaster and Corsini (1982) identify these as (1) direction, which derives from striving toward goals and (2) activity, in which individuals constantly and consistently move toward goals. They maintain that a major part of the social context in which individuals create their personalities and their subjective goals is within the family unit. They further state that: "Within any family there are parental expectations for each child based on the child's sex and birth order" (p. 83). Thomas and Marchant (1983) maintain that children tend to live up to the expectations implicit in the roles given by the parents. Christensen (1983) states that: "Each ordinal position offers the child who occupies it a different vantage point for interpreting life. . . . Some similarities of personality as a result of birth order have been noted over the years by many psychologists" (p. 6). Additionally, the Adlerian theory, which views people as "socially embedded in interacting social systems" (Thomas and Marchant 1983, 10), takes the position that brothers and sisters affect each other's personality.

Individual Psychology sees personality as being a combination of heredity, social experiences, and the individual's interpretation of both. Manaster and Corsini identify birth order position [the sequence in which one is born into a family] in the family constellation as a "soft" determinant of personality; in other words, an influencing factor in an individual's choice of goal striving. They state that: "The concept of soft determinism means statistical probability" (Manaster and Corsini 1982, 86). Forer summarizes the historical importance and significance of birth order position, harking back to the work of Sir Frances Galton. In 1874, Galton concluded, on the basis of the disproportionately large number of only and firstborn sons whom he found among eminent English scientists, that parents often treat an only or firstborn child differently from later borns. Generally, they have much higher expectations for the only or firstborn. This was intensified by the fact that Britain, at that time, still followed the legal custom of bestowing the family fortune and responsibility on the firstborn son after the father died (Forer 1977, 5).

Manaster and Corsini summarize the research literature and identify the following descriptions of birth order position.

1. Firstborns achieve more than do later borns, especially in intellectual areas (Altus 1966).
2. Firstborns show greater need for affiliation than do later borns, who are more independent (Adams 1972).
3. Later borns tend to have more empathy with others than do firstborns (Stotland, Sherman, and Shaver 1971).
4. Firstborns tend to generalize more than do later borns, who tend to be more specific (Harris 1964).
5. Firstborns tend to be more fearful than are later borns (Collard 1968).
6. Firstborns are more likely to be influenced by authority and to be affected by public opinion than later borns (Becker, Lerner, & Carroll 1964).

Recent literature on the effects of birth categories includes work in the area of interpersonal characteristics and achievement motivation. Falbo (1981) looks at the correlation between birth category and the personality characteristics of achievement and interpersonal orientation. She studies four types of sibling situations, which she identifies as *birth categories* (p. 121): only, first, middle, and last borns. She finds that birth category effects in achievement orientation occur along with competitiveness and educational aspirations; the effects vary by gender on the work scale (on which women score higher than men) and on competitiveness and educational aspiration (on which men score higher than women) (p. 126). Overall, firstborns score higher on the competitiveness scale than any of the other categories; Falbo states that "the presence of siblings could account for the differences in competitiveness" (p. 129). Additionally, Falbo maintains that "the powerfulness of the gender effects found in this study are testimony to the importance of gender for personality development" and "are largely consistent with those found previously" (p. 130).

Snell et al. (1986) investigate birth categories, achievement motivation configurations, and gender effects. The results of this investigation support their predictions that there would be both ordinal position effects and gender effects, and that "women's and men's birth category position is related to particular achievement motivation constellations" (p. 435). For example, male only children have a low work-high competitiveness profile, while female only children have a high work-high competitiveness profile. They find a statistically significant relationship between gender and work, "due to the greater percentage of women in the high work group, opposed to the lower percentage of males in the high work condition" (p. 433). They surmise that their findings of work-gender and competitiveness-gender interactions are consistent with previous research results.

Jordan et al. (1982) analyze the relationship between seven birth order schemes and eight achievement variables, finding that "achievement measures were shown to be related to birth order, provided the categories include information about the sex of the subject and sex of the siblings" (p. 257). They also note that "sex is closely related to achievement motivation" (p. 258) and that the family position heightens this effect. Male only children have the absolute highest means, indicating that they have exaggerated masculine achievement characteristics. Snell et al. conclude that "sex and the placement of siblings were found to be related to achievement measures" (p. 259).

Birth Order Summary

The research literature provides a clear indication of the importance of birth order. It has been identified as having an effect on the achievement/motivation of individuals (Falbo 1981; Snell et al. 1986; and Jordan et al. 1982) and is considered to be a major factor in personality development. Additionally, gender and the gender of siblings is a variable closely related to and interacting with birth order.

SELF-ESTEEM

Rosenberg (1965), in his study of the development of adolescent self-image, defines self-esteem as "a positive or negative attitude toward a particular object, namely, the self" (p. 30). He bases his theory, in part, on ideas proposed by William James: "That the normal *provocative* of self feeling is one's actual success or failure, and the good or bad actual position one holds in the world" ([1890] cited in Rosenberg and Pearlin 1978). Rosenberg defines high self-esteem to mean that "The individual respects himself, considers himself worthy, recognizes his limitations, and expects to grow and improve" (p. 31); by contrast, low self-esteem "implies self-rejection, self-dissatisfaction, self-contempt. The individual lacks respect for the self he observes, and he wishes it were otherwise" (p. 31). Wylie (1979) identifies self-esteem as "over-all self-regard" (p. 4), along with such other global constructs as self-acceptance and self-favorability.

Rosenberg and Pearlin (1978) suggest that the principles of self-esteem development, social comparison, reflected appraisals, self-perception theory, and psychological centrality apply equally to adults and children. In their study of comparisons of self-esteem between adults and children, they maintain that any noticeable difference found is not attributable to age; "The differential association of social class to self-esteem for children and adults stems from the different social experiences and psychological interpretations associated with this structural fact" (p. 73).

In her review of the theories of self-concept and age, Wylie (1979) confirms Rosenberg's work and summarizes the "general assumption that the person throughout the life span attempts to maintain or enhance his or her self-regard" (p. 9). She concludes that the relationship between age and self-regard is nonexistent.

"When such differences are found, they need to be replicated and possible sources of them [differences] other than age per se should be explored" (p. 33).

Grayson (1986) acknowledges the widespread influence of the self-esteem motive in the field of Individual Psychology. He states that for adults in therapy, "disavowing the past serves as a means of protecting and enhancing self-esteem" (p. 332). He contends that "this safeguarding mechanism fits within Adler's forward oriented theory and Rosenberg's work on self-esteem" (p. 337). Grayson cites Rosenberg's contention that individuals protect their self-esteem by placing the greatest importance on their assets and the least importance on their "subjective weaknesses" (p. 331).

Wylie's review of research related to self-concept/self-esteem and of the variables of sex, family, and achievement finds no support for differences in self-esteem. She maintains that although many theorists suggest that females compare unfavorably with males in overall self-regard, "The evidence from studies involving well-known instruments fails to support a relationship between sex and over-all self-regard" (p. 273). Furthermore, studies using the family and achievement variables likewise find no support for differences in self-esteem. This lack of support may be attributable to methodological weaknesses and inconsistencies in the research (p. 372).

Self-esteem Summary

The review of self-esteem literature indicates that the variables of gender, age, family, and achievement produce no empirically supported evidence of effect on the level of self-esteem. The evidence points to the possibility of an effect of personal interpretation as an impacting variable on self-esteem (Wylie 1979; Rosenberg and Pearlin 1978; Grayson 1986).

SUMMARY

This chapter has summarized research in the following areas: career development theory; career development of women; definitions of success; characteristics of successful career women;

ordinal positions; achievement/motivation and self-esteem. The major findings include:

1. Career development theories, norms for standardized career tests, and interest inventories were all based on a primary population of white Anglo-Saxon males.

2. The career development of women began to be separately researched in the 1960s. Long-term assumptions of why women worked were questioned and revisions were suggested.

3. Distinct differences related to gender and to socialization influences make it inappropriate to apply the career development theory formulated for males to females.

4. Of the varied definitions of success, one of the common themes found in the literature is the importance of visibility or recognition as a component of success.

5. The literature indicates that successful career women share some common characteristics, such as determination, perseverance, and being hardworking. Furthermore, women in male-dominated careers have additional characteristics in common, such as being more independent and aggressive, in contrast with career women in general.

6. The literature on achievement/motivation indicates that while male/female differences have been postulated, the focus of the research has been primarily on the Anglo-Saxon male population. As with the career development theories, the achievement/motivation measures for males do not necessarily work well for females.

7. Birth order has been identified as having an effect on the achievement/motivation of individuals.

8. The research on self-esteem does not provide any empirically supported evidence that the variables of gender, age, family, and/or achievement have an effect on the level of the self-esteem of individuals.

Chapter 3

Methods

The purpose of this study is to (1) identify the personal characteristics that successful career women have in common across career fields; (2) consider differences in achievement/motivation and self-esteem between occupational fields, as well as other independent variables; (3) provide demographic profiles of successful career women in general; and (4) contribute to the general body of knowledge about women and careers.

This chapter describes the population and sample, the overall design, the instrumentation, the procedures, and the data analysis.

POPULATION AND SAMPLE

Population

The population for this study consisted of career women who had been recognized as successful by their peers, by virtue of having been either nominated for recognition or selected by a professional organization, civic group, women's recognition event, or their employers. The criterion of recognition as an indicator of success was used for the following reasons: to identify a large portion of the population of working women; to provide the opportunity to include all career fields and career levels; and because recognition is a component of much of the literature on successful career women.

The population was identified by writing to businesses, civic clubs, and organizations in one large urban city in the Southwest and requesting the names and addresses of those women whom they had recognized by nominating for an award in the past five years (Appendix A). The total population identified produced an n of 528.

Sample

The sample consisted of a total of 249 women who returned usable questionnaires (Appendix C) within the time specified in the cover letter (Appendix B). An additional 66 questionnaires were accounted for (but not used) in the analysis. They consisted of: 29 undeliverable, 15 retired, 12 full-time volunteers, and 10 with insufficient data, rendering their questionnaires unusable. The sample represented a 57 percent return rate after a single mailing.

INSTRUMENTS

In order to gather information about successful career women, a questionnaire and interview format needed to be developed. The questionnaire and cover letter used information from a variety of sources including Hennig and Jardim (1977), Zimmerman (1983), and Rosenberg (1965). Several questionnaires relating to career women were reviewed. Although these instruments provided insight and some specific information, none was completely appropriate for this study. A questionnaire (Appendix C) was designed specifically for this study. The several sections included (1) requests for demographic data, (2) rating scales, (3) rank order questions, and (4) open-ended questions to test the hypotheses.

The self-esteem scale (Rosenberg 1965) was included as questions 12 to 21. The achievement/motivation scale (Myers, 1965) was modified and identified by questions 22 to 28; the list of personal characteristics (Zimmerman 1983) were identified in question 29. The interview questions (Appendix D) were also designed specifically for this study to provide information for descriptive narrative, including information on career success, career paths, and mentoring. Both instruments were designed to identify personal characteristics of successful career women; to establish levels of achievement/motivation and self-esteem; and to yield a general profile of the successful career woman.

The questionnaire and interview format were field tested by having three career women complete the questionnaire and two career women participate in the interview in order to provide feedback regarding specific items, clarity, and direction of the instruments. The instruments were revised based upon the critique by the career women and were used in the revised form.

PROCEDURE

Selection of Subjects (Questionnaire)

Businesses, civic clubs, educational and other institutions, and organizations were contacted by letter. They were requested to furnish the names and addresses of those women whom they had recognized by nominating for an award within the past five years. The responses were compiled, and duplicates and the names of deceased were eliminated (n = 528). The master list of names was then numbered sequentially; the questionnaires were numbered with the corresponding sequence of numbers. This procedure provided the identification necessary for a random selection of respondents for personal interviews while it protected the anonymity of the respondents. The questionnaire and cover letter were mailed to the identified population, along with a stamped, addressed envelope to be used to return the completed questionnaire.

Selection of Subjects (Interview)

Using random tables in Gay (1976), a random selection of 25 subjects was made from the total sample for possible interviewing. Only those numbers whose questionnaires had been returned were used. The interview group was contacted individually by telephone and letter (Appendix E) to inquire about willingness to continue to participate in the study. If the individuals were willing, appointments for the interviews were set.

The interviews were conducted in an office setting and generally lasted about one hour. Each interview opened with the following statement:

___(first name)___ , you have been randomly selected to be interviewed, as stated in the cover letter of the Career Women Questionnaire. This interview is to provide more in-depth information about career women in general. The information will be used for research and publication only. You will not be identified personally. Is it all right with you if I tape the interview?

The responses to the interview questions were tape-recorded and then transcribed to allow for comparison and summary analysis.

RESEARCH HYPOTHESES

The continuing upward trend of women working has generated increasing interest and research on women and careers. Most research has tended to isolate specific groups of career women (particularly those in the non-traditional fields) or to compare career women with men or with college students.

Questions remain about career women in general, inclusive of career fields and career levels. The following hypotheses address some of these questions:

1. Successful career women will have a high degree of self-esteem as identified by Rosenberg's self-esteem scale.
2. Successful career women across career fields will have characteristics in common with successful career women within given career fields, including

   Arts: Literary, visual, and performing.

   Business: Entrepreneurial, managerial, and non-managerial.

   Education: Administration and instruction.

   Government: Political and military.

   Health services: Medical, mental, and social services.

Legal: Attorney, judicial, and law enforcement.

Media: Audio, visual, and written.

Religion: Pastoral or educational.

Nontraditional: Any profession that is predominantly male.

3. There will be differences in both achievement/motivation and self-esteem among ordinal positions, between income levels, and between career levels of management and nonmanagement.

4. There will be no difference in achievement/motivation and self-esteem between occupational fields or between ethnic groups.

5. There will be a positive relationship between self-esteem scores and achievement/motivation scores and the variables of perception of success, financial compensation satisfaction, and emotional compensation satisfaction.

6. There will be no relationship between self-esteem and achievement/motivation and the variables of age and income.

Additional Research Questions

1. What self-reported factors of achievement/motivation and self-esteem are shared by successful career women?

2. What are the self-reported personal characteristics of successful career women?

3. What are the three major components of success as defined by successful career women?

DATA ANALYSIS

Statistical Procedure

In order to test the hypotheses and to provide general information about career women across career fields and levels, the following statistical procedures were utilized.

1. *Descriptive:* The descriptive reporting (Gay 1976) includes an overall profile of the successful career woman. The profile

includes the number of years in the career field, age category, ethnicity, mentor information, definition of success category, and financial support information.

2. *Correlation: Pearson's* r: Pearson's product moment coefficient (Gay 1976) was used to determine what, if any, relationship exists between the variables of (1) self-esteem and (2) achievement/motivation and each of the following variables: age, perception of success, financial compensation satisfaction, emotional compensation satisfaction, and income category.

3. *Factor analysis:* A factor analysis procedure (Glass and Hopkins 1984) was used to identify subscales of subjects' personal characteristics and subscales of their self-esteem and achievement/motivation. In addition to providing information by identifying them, the three subscales were also used as dependent variables for the analysis of variance.

4. *ANOVA:* Using the self-esteem, achievement/motivation, and personal characteristics subscales as separate dependent variables, a separate analysis of variance (Glass and Hopkins 1984) was done for the following independent variables: occupational field, ordinal position, marital status, ethnic group, and income category, in order to identify any differences.

Chapter 4

Results

This chapter presents the findings produced by the methods described in chapter 3. A description of the population and the profiles of the characteristics of successful career women appears first. Then each hypothesis is discussed separately. The additional research questions are addressed. Finally, a summary of the information from the 23 personal interviews is presented.

The following data were based on information provided by 249 subjects, all career women who returned usable questionnaires. These career women represented 50 percent of the identified population of 528. An additional 66 subjects were accounted for but not used in the analysis for the following reasons: 29 were not located; 15 were retired; 12 were full-time volunteers in the community; and 10 had sufficient data missing to render the questionnaires unusable.

POPULATION DESCRIPTION

The questionnaire included questions whose answers provided general demographic information about the population of career women. This information included age category, educational level, ordinal position, marital status, ethnic category, and income level.

The sample for this study (n = 249) was composed of career women whose number of years in their field ranged from one to

41 years; the number of years in their current position ranged from one to 34 years. There were 177 subjects in management positions and 72 in nonmanagement positions. All educational levels were represented, as were all age categories and ordinal positions. In terms of ethnicity, the sample included 193 Anglos, 18 Mexican-Americans, 15 Native Americans, 14 Blacks, seven Others (nonspecified), and two Asians. The marital status representation was nine single, 56 divorced, 124 married, 22 remarried, 30 never-married, and eight widowed. These categories represent the different perspectives women have in defining their marital status, as identified in the field development of the questionnaire. The number of children ranged from zero to six (Tables 1 through 6).

Over half the women (154) indicated that they have or have had mentors; of those, 15 said they had had both male and female mentors. Of the remainder, 102 stated that they had had only male mentors, while 79 had had only female mentors. In addition, 95 women indicated they have had no mentor. In terms of success, 74 ranked themselves as extremely successful, 150 as successful, and 25 as moderately successful. No one ranked herself as unsuccessful (Tables 7 and 8).

As to financial compensation, 22 women indicated that they were extremely well compensated for their work, with 188 reporting themselves well or adequately compensated and 39 indicating that they were not compensated enough (Table 9). On the emotional compensation indicators 156 stated they were extremely well or well compensated emotionally, 57 adequately compensated, and 35 not compensated enough emotionally for their work (Table 10). Their annual incomes ranged from $20,000 or less to over $101,000 (Table 11). Roughly half the women (123) indicated that they provided the primary support for themselves and/or their families, while 76 indicated an equal sharing of the primary support, and 49 were not the primary support of themselves and/or their families (Table 12).

SUCCESSFUL CAREER WOMAN PROFILE

Once the demographic information was compiled and averaged, the following profile was composed (Table 13). The profile of the subjects indicates that the mean number of years in their field was 13.26 (SD = 8.29); the mean number of years in their current position was 5.60 (SD = 15.18), with 72.0 percent in management positions. Of the subjects, 62.2 percent had earned either a bachelor's or a master's degree. The majority, 68.0 percent, were between the ages of 36 and 55; 51.4 percent were in the only or oldest category (31.7 percent were oldest). In terms of marital status, 58.0 percent were married or remarried; the women had an average of 1.62 children. The large majority of the subjects, 77.5 percent, were Anglo.

There were 61.8 percent who stated that they have or have had a mentor; 41.0 percent had had only male mentors. Sixty percent ranked themselves as successful, with an additional 29.7 percent ranking themselves extremely successful.

The majority of the subjects, 55.0 percent, stated that they were either extremely well or well compensated financially for their work, and 62.7 percent indicated they were emotionally compensated for their work either extremely well or well. Nearly four-fifths of the subjects, 79.9 percent, were either the primary financial supporter (49.4 percent) or shared that responsibility equally. The most frequent income category was $21,000-$40,000 as checked by 50.2 percent of the subjects (Table 11).

DEFINITIONS OF SUCCESS RANKING

The subjects rank ordered 12 listed definitions of success, which included "becoming an authority in your occupation" and "having a title and job description indicating high responsibility." The mean rank for the subjects' ranking of the definitions of success (as identified in question 10) are indicated in Table 14. The three most highly ranked definitions of success were identified as: first, becoming an authority in your occupation, which had a mean rank of 2.40; second, obtaining recognition from others in your job, with a mean rank of 3.74; and third, contributing to the welfare of friends or personal acquaintances, with a mean rank of 4.48.

OCCUPATIONAL CATEGORY DISTRIBUTION

The subjects were categorized by occupation. Table 15 indicates the frequency and percent of subjects by occupational category.

The distribution of subjects by occupational field shows that the three largest groups were: the business category with 91 subjects (36.5 percent), health services with 52 subjects (20.9 percent), and education with 36 subjects (14.5 percent).

SELF-DESCRIPTIVE WORDS RANKING

The subjects were given a list of 38 descriptive words and asked to identify to what degree each word described herself and related to her career success. A Likert-type scale was used and ranged from 1 (not at all) to 5 (extremely). The mean rank for the descriptive words chosen by the subjects in question 29 is identified in Table 16.

The self-descriptive words most often chosen by the subjects out of a list of 38 words were: responsible, with a mean of 4.63 (SD = .54); competent, with a mean of 4.41 (SD = .59), and hard-working, with a mean of 4.41 (SD = .66). Committed had a mean of 4.40 (SD = .62); sincere, a mean of 4.38 (SD = .66); persevering and motivated shared a mean of 4.34 (SD = .67); and action-oriented had a mean of 4.34 (SD = .69). The words chosen least often were: aggressive, with a mean of 3.17 (SD = 1.09) and ruthless, with a mean of 1.61 (SD = .80).

SELF-ESTEEM

The questionnaire included an adaptation of Rosenberg's scale of 10 questions—five positively stated and five negatively stated—to measure self-esteem. The mean ranks for the self-esteem measures, questions 12 through 21, are identified in Table 17.

The most strongly agreed-with statements were: having a number of good qualities, with a mean of 3.79 (SD = .41); feeling like a person of worth, at least equal to others, with a mean of 3.74 (SD = .45); and being able to do things as well as most others, with a mean of 3.55 (SD = .59). The most strongly disagreed-with statements were: being inclined to feel like a failure, with a mean of 1.20 (SD = .43); not having much to be proud of, with a mean of 1.28 (SD = .63); and at times thinking I am no good at all, with a mean of 1.56 (SD = .72).

ACHIEVEMENT/MOTIVATION

The achievement/motivation scale, adapted from Myer's educational model, consisted of seven questions. The mean ranks for the achievement/motivation measure, questions 22 through 28, are identified in Table 18.

The most strongly agreed-with statements were: I really want to succeed, with a mean of 3.53 (SD = .52), and my friends think of me as a hard worker, with a mean of 3.50 (SD = .52). The most strongly disagreed-with statements were: other interests keep me from being exemplary in my field, with a mean of 1.72 (SD = .62) and my family commitments keep me from being exemplary in my field, with a mean of 1.81 (SD = .71).

HYPOTHESIS ONE

The first hypothesis, that successful career women will have a high degree of self-esteem as measured by Rosenberg's self-esteem scale, was addressed by studying responses to questions 12 through 21. The range of answers was 4 (strongly agree) to 1 (strongly disagree). A mean of 2.0 indicated a moderate level of self-esteem. The hypothesis was supported to the degree that the overall mean for career women's self-esteem was 3.49. A z test was computed to ascertain the level of significance of the self-esteem mean. The results strongly support significance.

HYPOTHESIS TWO

The second hypothesis was that successful career women as a group will have characteristics in common with successful career women within the given career fields, including art, business, education, government, health services, legal, media, religion, and nontraditional. This hypothesis was addressed by comparing the mean ranks of the self-descriptive words in question 29 for the overall population and the mean ranks of the words chosen by each of the identified career fields. The results appear in Table 19.

The hypothesis was supported by the data. These showed that seven out of the nine occupational groups identified the same descriptive word, responsible, as the number one choice most frequently. Only one occupational category, religion, did not have this word among the top six choices (Table 20).

The occupational categories of religion and nontraditional were less like the total self-descriptive characteristics than any of the other occupational categories.

HYPOTHESIS THREE

The third hypothesis was that there will be a difference in both self-esteem and achievement/motivation in terms of the variables of ordinal position, income levels, and between career levels of management and nonmanagement. This hypothesis was addressed by the use of a one-way analysis of variance (ANOVA) to identify any differences. The one-way ANOVA for ordinal position and self-esteem indicates that ordinal position has a significant effect on self-esteem, with $F = 4.6728$ (df = 3), $p = .0034$ at the .01 level. The Scheffe post hoc procedure identified group 4, the youngest ordinal position, as significantly different from groups 1 and 2, the only and oldest ordinal positions.

The one-way ANOVA for ordinal position and achievement/ motivation indicates that ordinal position has a significant effect on achievement/motivation as well, with $F = 2.7419$ (df = 3), $p = .0439$ at .05 level. The Scheffe procedure identified group 1, the only ordinal position, as having a higher level of achievement/motivation than any other ordinal position.

The results of the one-way ANOVA for self-esteem and income level indicate that income level had no main effect on self-esteem. The Scheffe procedure was not run, since there was no significance. The one-way ANOVA for achievemnent/motivation and income level indicates a trend for income level to have an effect on achievement/motivation, with $F = 1.9536$ (df = 5), $p = .0865$. The results indicate that there were no significant effects at the .100 level.

The one-way ANOVA for self-esteem and management level results indicate that management level had no main effect on self-esteem. There were no significant differences between groups at the .100 level. The results of the one-way ANOVA for achievement/motivation and management level indicate that management level had no main effect on achievement/motivation either. There was no significant difference between the means of the groups at the .100 level.

In other words, hypothesis three—that there will be a difference in both achievement/motivation and self-esteem among ordinal positions; between income levels; and between career levels of management and nonmanagement—was partially supported. Ordinal position was the only variable shown to have a significant effect on both self-esteem and achievement/motivation. There was a trend toward significance in the effect of income level on achievement/motivation, but no main effect of income level on self-esteem. There was no main effect of management level on either self-esteem or achievement/motivation.

HYPOTHESIS FOUR

The fourth hypothesis, that there will be no difference in achievement/motivation and self-esteem between occupational fields or between ethnic groups, was studied by use of the one-way analysis of variance (ANOVA) to identify any differences.

The results of the one-way ANOVA between achievement/motivation and occupational fields indicate that occupational field had no main effect on achievement/motivation. There was no support for this portion of the hypothesis.

The results of the one-way ANOVA between self-esteem and the nine occupational fields indicate there was a significant effect between groups at the .05 level with F = 2.0558 (df = 8), p = .0410. The Scheffe procedure identified the nontraditional group (n = 13) as having the highest self-esteem mean of 3.66; the second highest mean (3.58) was in the health services group (n = 51). The lowest self-esteem mean (3.20) was found in the legal group (n = 13).

The results of the one-way ANOVA between self-esteem and achievement/motivation on the one hand, and the variable of ethnicity on the other, indicate no significant main effect for ethnicity at the .100 level.

Thus, the fourth hypothesis, that there will be no difference in achievement/motivation and self-esteem between occupational fields or between ethnic groups, was supported, with the exception of slight differences in the levels of self-esteem between occupational groups.

HYPOTHESIS FIVE

The fifth hypothesis, that there will be a positive relationship between self-esteem and achievement/motivation scores on the one hand and the variables of perception of success, financial compensation satisfaction, and emotional compensation satisfaction on the other, was studied by using a Pearson product moment correlation to determine correlation coefficients and levels of significance.

There was a positive relationship between self-esteem and perception of success, with $r = .3687$ at the .001 level. There was no relationship between self-esteem and financial compensation satisfaction, but there was a positive relationship between self-esteem and emotional compensation satisfaction, with $r = .2859$ at the .001 level (Table 21).

There was no relationship between achievement/motivation and any of the variables of perception of success, financial compensation satisfaction, or emotional compensation satisfaction (Table 22).

Therefore, the fifth hypothesis, that there will be a positive relationship between self-esteem or achievement/motivation scores and the variables of perception of success, financial compensation satisfaction, and emotional compensation satisfaction, was partially supported. Self-esteem seemed to be positively related to a higher degree of perceived success and to a higher emotional compensation satisfaction level. There was no significant relationship between self-esteem or achievement/ motivation and financial compensation satisfaction.

HYPOTHESIS SIX

The sixth hypothesis, that there will be no relationship between self-esteem or achievement/motivation and the variables of age or income, was studied by using a Pearson product moment to determine correlation coefficients and levels of significance.

The hypothesis was supported. There was no identifiable relationship between self-esteem and the variables of age and income, nor was there a relationship between achievement/ motivation and the variables of age and income (see Table 22).

ADDITIONAL RESEARCH QUESTIONS

Question 1 sought to identify self-reported factors of achievement/motivation and self-esteem shared by successful career women. It was investigated by use of a factor analysis procedure. Three factors were identified in the analysis (Table 23). The two factors of self-esteem and achievement/motivation validated the questions used in the questionnaire. The third was labeled a "discouraged" factor, because it was loaded by discouraging or negative questions.

Question 2 looked for the self-reported personal characteristics of successful career women and was investigated by sorting the self-descriptive words through a factor analysis procedure. Eight factors were identified (Table 24). These factors were labeled according to the constructs that they seem to identify (Table 25).

Question 3 sought to identify the three main components of success as defined by the subjects and was investigated through question 11.

The subjects were asked to write their own definitions of success. Fifty women chose not to respond. There were thus 199 women (79 percent of the sample) who wrote responses. These responses were evaluated and then placed in the following categories: receiving recognition; achieving personal goals; being respected by others; enjoying my work; having a lot of money; being of service to others; having freedom or independence; doing a good job; achieving a higher position; having a balanced life; contributing to society; continual learning; being very competent; significant accomplishment; marriage and family; receiving approval from others; being happy; surviving in the marketplace; and personal growth.

The most frequent definition given was achieving personal goals with 18 percent. The second most frequent definition, contributing to society, accounted for 14.6 percent of the responses, while the third, doing a good job, drew 10.6 percent (see Table 26).

The self-esteem and achievement/motivation constructs were validated with the factor analysis procedure. The personal characteristics of successful career women produced eight factors through this procedure. The self-reported definitions of success yielded some (new) categories of success that had not been included in the questionnaire list.

RESULTS OF PERSONAL INTERVIEWS

The subjects for the personal interviews were randomly selected from the population identified. Only those who had returned a completed questionnaire were considered for interviewing purposes. The interviews were conducted in an office setting and generally lasted about one hour. They were tape recorded in order to provide accurate quotations and information for analysis.

PROFILE OF INTERVIEWEES

Twenty-three career women agreed to be interviewed (two refused to participate). All of the occupational fields were represented, with the exceptions of arts and media. The women averaged 17.6 years in their field. The mean age was 45.1, and 78 percent were Anglo. Sixty percent were married; the average number of children was 1.4. Two ordinal positions, oldest and youngest, tied at 30 percent for highest representation. There were 65 percent who stated they had had a mentor; of that group, 53 percent had had only female mentors. Those who provided their own and/or their family's primary financial support accounted for 52 percent of the women interviewed (see Table 27).

DECISION TO ENTER CAREER FIELD

When asked how they had decided to enter their career field, six of the women interviewed gave responses that reflected traditional socialization for females. One respondent stated, "I thought at that time [of finishing high school] that I had three choices: to be a teacher, a secretary, or a nurse." These six women either chose what was considered a traditional female occupation or followed a female family tradition. Four of these six remained in the traditional field. The other two made career changes and were now working in other fields. All but one of this group had advanced further than they had anticipated at the beginning of their careers.

Five women interviewed had entered their career field "by accident." They were willing to risk something new or different, as stated by one woman in a nontraditional field:

I got into this just by accident. I have a degree in education and was a teacher for a few years. I realized the second day that I *really* did not want to do that! When we moved because of my husband's job, there were no full-time jobs available so I went to an employment agency and they sent me to the telephone company.

For a long time I said I was a teacher who just happens to be working for Mountain Bell. But now I'm a Mountain Bell manager [engineering and construction department] who used to be a teacher. I had no intention of going to work for a utility, or even then, had no thoughts of going into management. *Things like that were out of my realm of achieving expectations.*

Four women had sought something challenging or different in a career. All of these women were in career fields dominated primarily by males. Three of the four were now in professional careers that required extensive education: engineering, medicine, and law.

Three more women decided to enter their career field based on volunteer experiences that they had had as high school students. Two of these entered their field out of economic necessity, for either themselves or their families.

The final three women interviewed had varied reasons for entering their career field. The reasons ranged from the death of a spouse to the current atmosphere of social change (see Table 28).

CAREER PATTERNS

The interviewees were asked to describe their career histories. The histories were then evaluated and placed in the following five categories:

1. Continuous occupational field, planned entry.
2. Continuous occupational field, unplanned entry, upwardly mobile (includes those who entered the occupational field "by accident"; however, once in the field, they made a conscious effort to be upwardly mobile in their career).
3. Continuous occupational field, unplanned entry (includes those who have had no consistent career path).
4. Re-entry career (coming from the career of homemaker).
5. Career change (involved changing occupational fields).

The majority of those interviewed, 74 percent, had spent their working time in a continuous occupational field. Only 35 percent of those, however, had planned their career and career path. The other 39 percent had stayed in the same occupational field, even though their entry and career path was unplanned.

There were three re-entry women. These women entered their career field after spending their early adult years as home-makers and community volunteers. Their reasons for entry into the paid occupational field ranged from losing a spouse through death or divorce to the desire for self-fulfillment.

Three of the women interviewed had made major career changes. One woman completely changed occupational fields, while the other two had changed the focus of their careers. They chose to refocus on their family lives and had constructed their work so that their spouses and families received their primary consideration (Table 29).

FACTORS HELPFUL IN CAREER

When the women were asked what had been most helpful in their careers, 48 percent acknowledged their mentors. Personal characteristics were frequently cited at 39 percent and were followed closely by the influence or expectations of parents at 31 percent. Other positive factors included helpful college professors, supportive friends, meeting challenges, continuing to learn and grow, enjoying their work, supportive husbands, the women's movement, having full responsibility for a family, and helpful high school counselors (Table 30).

The personal characteristics that the women listed as helpful included their own desire to achieve, having a positive outlook or high energy, being flexible, even-tempered, highly motivated, creative, enthusiastic, persevering, a problem solver, and working hard.

PERCEIVED CHARACTERISTICS OF
SUCCESSFUL CAREER WOMEN

The interviewees were asked to describe the characteristics of other career women whom they perceived to be successful. Some of the women had difficulty addressing this question. One stated, "I never even thought about that!" The description most frequently used for other successful career women was as achievers or as having a strong drive. Next came being self-confident and setting goals, followed by being organized, self-directed, and contributing to or helping others. Additional attributes included taking risks, having a positive outlook, getting involved in the community, working hard, persevering, desiring to make changes, having a supportive spouse, making good decisions, being energetic, knowledgeable, tough, focused, enthusiastic, fair, honest, intelligent, encouraging, agreeable, androgynous, analytical, ambitious, determined, politically aware, and finally, enjoying their work and meeting challenges (Table 31).

CAREER GOALS AND GOAL SETTING

When asked about goal setting and their career goals, most of the women, 57 percent, could not verbalize specific career goals at this point in their careers. They seemed to be in a maintenance position with regard to career goals, as one professional woman stated:

I think I have [set goals] in the past. I don't know that I'm so actively involved in that right now. I might be in this job for the next 30 years, pretty much like I am now. . . . There's just sort of a different quality to them [career goals] as compared to goals when you are 20.

Thirteen percent of the women were actively setting specific career goals, as summed up by one woman: "At this point, I have lots of them [goals]. I would like to be a department head and to go into upper management." The remainder of the women were either currently revising their career goals (two), planning for retirement (two), focusing more on their families (two), or not setting goals at all (two).

For the most part, the process of goal setting was very flexible and informal. Rarely did anyone state that she set specific three- or five-year goals. One woman stated:

It's not very formalized. Most of the time it would be thinking about something I want to accomplish. Most of it stays in my head. I've never had a five-year, three-year, ten-year kind of plan. I would say that I am much more of an opportunist than a planner. I really seize whatever's in front of me, and I put a lot of energy into making things happen.

SELF-RATINGS OF SUCCESS

The women were asked to rate their career success on a scale of 0 to 10, with 10 being extremely successful. Only two women rated themselves at 10, and two rated themselves at 9. The largest share of the women, 11, rated themselves at 8. The most frequent rationale for that rating was, "I'm not finished yet."

Most of the women who rated themselves lower than 8 did so because they felt a strong need to do more in their career for advancement or for the accomplishment of their own goals, such as learning more, publishing more, or increasing their professional visibility (Table 32).

DEFINITIONS OF CAREER SUCCESS

Each of the women was asked to define career success. Over half, 52 percent, answered "Achieving one's personal goals." "Enjoying one's work" at 49 percent was a close second. Other responses included "having self-satisfaction" (22 percent) and "receiving peer or community recognition" (17 percent) (Table 33).

ADVICE FOR ASPIRING WOMEN

When asked what advice they would give to other women who aspired to enter their career field, the overwhelming response, 65 percent, was an emphatic "know yourself, know what you want!" The second most frequent response, 57 percent, was "prepare yourself, get the necessary credentials." The third most frequent response, 35 percent, was to "promote yourself and your work" (Table 34).

SUMMARY

The majority of the successful career women in this study (72 percent) were in management positions, were married (58 percent), and had a mentor (62 percent). Nearly one-half of these women (49.4 percent) were providing the primary financial support for themselves and/or their family. About two thirds, 68 percent, were from 36 to 55 years of age. At least half of the women (55 percent) said that they were well compensated financially for their work, while more, 63 percent, said they were well compensated emotionally.

The successful career women had a well-above-average level of self-esteem of 3.49 (2.0 being average). This finding supported hypothesis 1. Hypothesis 2 was also supported. Successful career women as a group had characteristics in common with successful career women within the identified career fields, with the exception of the women in the field of religion.

Only one variable, ordinal position, was shown to have a significant effect on both self-esteem and achievement/motivation. There was a positive trend toward significance of the effect of income level on achievement/motivation. These findings partially supported hypothesis 3.

Hypothesis 4 was supported. There were no main effects of ethnicity or occupational field on achievement/motivation. There was, however, a slight difference in the levels of self-esteem between occupational groups, with the nontraditional group having the highest self-esteem mean. Self-esteem also seemed to be positively related to a higher degree of perception of success and to a high level of emotional compensation satisfaction. This partially supports the fifth hypothesis.

The sixth hypothesis was likewise supported. There was no identifiable relationship between self-esteem and achievement/ motivation and the variables of age and income.

Eight factors were identified in the analysis of the self-reported personal characteristics of the successful career women. The first factor, accounting for the most variance, was labeled achievement-oriented. The subjects identified three main components of success as achieving one's personal goals, contributing to society, and doing a good job.

The successful career women interviewed closely matched the profile of the total subjects. The average age was 45.1, and 78 percent were Anglo. Arts and media were the only occupational fields not included. Sixty percent of the women were married, and over half of this group, 52 percent, provided the primary support for themselves and/or their families.

Only 35 percent of the women interviewed had a planned entry into their career field, although 74 percent had spent their working time continuously in one occupational field. These women identified mentors and their own personal characteristics, such as a desire to achieve and having a positive outlook, as being most helpful to them in their careers. Further, the most frequently perceived characteristic of other successful women was being an achiever or having a strong drive.

Most of the women interviewed did not seem to set strong, rigid goals. Those who did seemed to use a more informal process rather than a specific three-, five- or ten-year goal plan.

The most frequent definitions of career success identified by the women interviewed were achieving one's personal goals and enjoying one's work. The majority of these women, 45.5 percent, rated their level of success at 8 or 9, with 10 being extremely successful. Finally, their most frequent advice to women aspiring to enter their career field was "Know yourself, know what you want."

Table 1
Educational Level (Number of Respondents by Educational Category)

Educational Category	Number of Responses	Frequency (%)
High School	38	15.3
Associate Degree	21	8.4
Apprenticeship	3	1.2
Bachelors degree	74	29.7
Masters degree	81	32.5
Doctorate	30	12.0
Post-doctorate	1	.4
Missing information	1	.4

n = 249

Table 2
Age Distribution (Number of Respondents by Age Category)

Age Group	Number of Responses	Frequency (%)
25 - 35	47	18.9
36 - 45	101	40.6
46 - 55	69	27.7
56 - 65	25	10.0
65+	5	2.0
Missing information	2	.8

n = 249

Table 3
Ordinal Position (Number of Respondents by Ordinal Position Category)

Ordinal Position	Number of Responses	Frequency (%)
Only	49	19.7
Oldest	84	33.7
Middle	40	16.1
Youngest	42	16.8
Second of 2	34	13.7

n = 249

Table 4
Ethnic Distribution (Number of Respondents by Ethnic Group)

Ethnic Group	Number of Responses	Frequency (%)
Anglo	193	77.5
Mexican American	18	7.2
Native American	15	6.0
Black	14	5.6
Other	7	2.8
Asian	2	.8

n = 249

Table 5
Marital Status (Number of Respondents by Marital Category)

Marital Status	Number of Responses	Frequency (%)
Married	124	49.8
Divorced	56	22.5
Never Married	30	12.0
Remarried	22	8.8
Single	9	3.6
Widowed	8	3.2

n = 249

Table 6
Status Regarding Children (Number of Respondents by
Parenthood Status)

Number of Children	Number of Responses	Frequency (%)
0	73	29.3
1	48	19.3
2	58	23.3
3	31	12.4
4	20	8.0
5	7	2.8
6	6	2.4

n = 243

Table 7
Mentors (Number of Respondents by Mentor Category)

Mentor Status	Number of Responses	Frequency (%)
Have had no mentor	95	38.2
Have or have had a mentor	154	61.8
Have had both male and female mentors	15*	
Had only female mentors	79*	
Had only male mentors	102*	

n = 249

* Indicates both past and present mentors. Some women had
more than one mentor.

Table 8
Success Ranking (Number of Respondents by Success Rank)

Level of Success	Number of Responses	Frequency (%)
Extremely successful	74	29.7
Successful	150	60.2
Moderately successful	25	10.0

n = 249

Table 9
Financial Compensation Satisfaction (Number of Respondents by Financial Compensation Satisfaction Category)

Compensation Satisfaction	Number of Responses	Frequency (%)
Extremely well satisfied	22	8.8
Well satisfied	115	46.2
Adequately satisfied	73	29.3
Not enough satisfaction	39	15.7

n = 249

Table 10
Emotional Compensation Satisfaction (Number of Respondents by Emotional Compensation Satisfaction Category)

Satisfaction Level	Number of Responses	Frequency (%)
Extremely well satisfied	58	23.3
Well satisfied	98	39.4
Adequately satisfied	57	22.9
Not enough satisfaction	35	14.1

n = 248

Table 11
Income Level (Number of Respondents by Income Level Category)

Annual Income	Number of Responses	Frequency (%)
Up to $20,000	45	18.1
$21-40,000	125	50.2
$41-60,000	53	21.3
$61-80,000	10	4.0
$81-100,000	6	2.4
$101,000+	6	2.4
Missing information	4	1.6

n = 249

Table 12
Financial Support Providers (Number of Respondents by Financial Support Level Category)

Support Level	Number of Responses	Frequency (%)
Providing primary financial support for self/family	123	49.4
Equally sharing primary financial support for self/family	76	30.5
Not providing primary financial support for self/family	49	19.7

n = 248

Table 13
Successful Career Woman Profile (Means and Percentages
of Population's Demographic Characteristics)

Profile	Mean - Average
Number of years in their field	13.26 (SD = 8.29)
Number of years in current position	5.60 (SD = 5.18)
Management positions	72.0%
Educational level: Bachelor's or Master's degree	62.0%
Age: 36-55 years	68.0%
Ordinal position: only or oldest	51.0%
Currently married	58.0%
Number of children	1.62
Ethnic category: Anglo	77.5%
Has mentor	62.0%
Ranks self as successful	60.0%
Well compensated financially	55.0%
Well compensated emotionally	63.0%
Provides primary financial support	49.4%
Income range: $21-40,000	50.2%

Table 14
Definition of Success (Mean Rank)

Definition of Success	Mean	Standard Deviation
Becoming an authority in your occupation	2.40	2.27
Obtaining recognition from others in your job	3.74	2.42
Contributing to the welfare of friends or personal acquaintances	4.48	2.60
Developing a strong relationship with others on the job	5.18	2.79
Obtaining recognition from friends or others outside of work	5.43	1.98
Having a title and job description indicating high responsibility	6.66	3.13
Being well liked	6.73	2.43
Achieving a very high salary	6.84	3.06
Supervising volunteer organizations or community projects	7.09	2.94
Obtaining awards outside the organization	7.11	2.41
Acquiring large home or expensive real estate	10.56	1.86
Marrying one who has money/position	11.21	1.62

Ranking was 1 = high, to 12 = low

Table 15
Occupational Category (Number of Respondents by Occupational Category)

Occupational Field	Number of Responses	Frequency (%)
Arts	5	2.0
Business	91	36.5
Education	36	14.5
Government	23	9.2
Health services	52	20.9
Legal	13	5.2
Media	10	4.0
Religion	6	2.4
Non-traditional	13	5.2

n = 249

Table 16
Self-descriptive Words (Mean Rank of Self-descriptive Words of Subjects)

Descriptive Words	Mean	Standard Deviation	n
Responsible	4.63	.54	247
Competent	4.41	.59	249
Hardworking	4.41	.66	249
Committed	4.40	.62	247
Sincere	4.38	.66	247
Perseverance	4.34	.67	247
Motivated	4.34	.67	247
Action oriented	4.34	.69	249
Enthusiastic	4.33	.71	246
Leader	4.22	.72	245

Table 16 *(continued)*

Descriptive Words	Mean	Standard Deviation	n
Person oriented	4.20	.82	246
Mature	4.19	.66	246
High achiever	4.18	.76	249
Level headed	4.14	.69	245
Empathetic	4.14	.76	244
Challenged	4.13	.85	246
Kind	4.11	.73	246
Optimistic	4.11	.77	246
Warm	4.11	.79	246
Goal oriented	4.09	.82	246
Intelligent	4.06	.63	249
Knowledgeable	4.04	.64	248
Openminded	4.01	.67	247
Realistic	4.01	.72	246
Congenial	4.01	.76	246
Confident	3.97	.82	249
Self assured	3.90	.80	247
Organized	3.86	.96	247
Flexible	3.85	.70	247
Assertive	3.82	.86	247
Ambitious	3.79	.82	246
Analytic	3.78	.87	249
Competitive	3.60	1.00	249
Patient	3.42	.98	247
Academically oriented	3.41	.94	248
Calm	3.39	.96	246
Aggressive	3.17	1.09	245
Ruthless	1.61	.80	244

Table 17
Self-esteem Questions (Mean Rank of Self-esteem Items)

Measure	Mean Rank	SD	n
I feel I have a number of good qualities	3.79	.41	247
I feel I'm a person of worth, at least equal with others	3.74	.45	247
I am able to do things as well as most other people	3.55	.59	246
I take a positive attitude toward myself	3.45	.58	249
On the whole, I am satisfied with myself	3.25	.60	249
I certainly feel useless at times	1.92	.82	246
I wish I could have more respect for myself	1.83	.81	246
At times I think I am no good at all	1.56	.72	249
I feel I do not have much to be proud of	1.28	.63	247
I am inclined to feel that I am a failure	1.20	.43	247

Note: Measures were checked from Strongly Agree (4) to Strongly Disagree (1).

Table 18
Achievement/Motivation Questions (Mean Rank of Achievement/Motivation Items)

Measure	Mean Rank	SD	n
I really want to succeed	3.53	.52	248
My friends think of me as a hard worker	3.50	.52	248
Most of my superior/supervisors/clientele think of me as one of their hardest workers	3.29	.57	245
I am a harder worker on my job than the average career woman	3.04	.73	247
Other workers think of me as being too serious	2.38	.73	247
My family commitments keep me from being exemplary in my field	1.81	.71	249
Other interests keep me from being exemplary in my field	1.72	.67	248

Note: Measures were checked from Strongly Agree (4) to Strongly Disagree (1).

Table 19
Common Characteristics Comparison (Mean Rank of Self-descriptive Words by Occupational Category)

Descriptive	Arts	Bus.	Educ.	Gov't.	Hlth.Sv.	Legal	Media	Rel.	Non-Tr.	Total
Responsible	5.0	4.60	4.61	4.77	4.65	4.62	4.50	4.33	4.62	4.63
Competent	4.80	4.41	4.42	4.43	4.38	4.15	4.70	4.33	4.31	4.41
Hardworking	4.80	4.48	4.33	4.35	4.44	4.23	4.40	4.17	4.15	4.41
Committed	4.60	4.34	4.47	4.45	4.44	4.08	4.60	4.67	4.23	4.40
Sincere	4.60	4.36	4.50	4.32	4.42	4.15	4.40	4.67	4.23	4.38
Perseverence	4.20	4.36	4.49	4.00	4.44	4.15	4.40	4.17	4.23	4.34
Motivated	4.60	4.31	4.42	4.45	4.37	4.23	4.20	4.33	4.08	4.34
Action-oriented	4.00	4.36	4.28	4.61	4.44	4.08	4.20	3.83	4.23	4.34
Enthusiastic	4.40	4.34	4.40	4.09	4.35	4.00	4.40	4.50	4.46	4.33
Leader	4.00	4.28	4.21	4.27	4.25	3.92	4.20	4.17	4.15	4.22
Person-oriented	3.40	4.11	4.37	3.86	4.35	4.31	4.60	4.67	3.92	4.20
Mature	3.40	4.22	4.20	4.18	4.27	4.08	4.00	4.50	4.00	4.19

High achiever	4.20	4.21	4.17	4.04	4.27	4.08	4.20	3.83	4.23	4.18
Level headed	4.00	4.17	4.11	4.09	4.25	3.92	4.10	4.40	3.85	4.14
Empathetic	4.60	3.98	4.31	3.76	4.33	4.15	4.40	4.67	4.08	4.14
Challenged	4.40	4.06	4.22	4.09	4.21	4.23	4.20	4.17	3.85	4.13
Kind	4.40	3.97	4.11	4.05	4.27	4.08	4.40	4.50	4.15	4.11
Optimistic	3.80	4.11	4.28	3.95	4.19	3.92	3.70	4.00	4.15	4.11
Warm	3.80	4.00	4.09	3.91	4.29	4.15	4.20	4.50	4.31	4.11
Goal-oriented	3.60	4.15	4.11	4.09	4.13	3.92	4.30	3.50	4.00	4.09
Intelligent	4.20	3.99	4.06	3.96	4.25	3.85	4.00	4.00	4.15	4.06
Knowledgeable	4.40	3.97	4.06	3.96	4.13	4.15	4.10	4.17	3.85	4.04
Openminded	4.20	4.03	3.83	4.18	4.06	3.85	4.20	3.83	3.85	4.01
Realistic	3.60	4.04	3.86	4.09	4.04	3.92	4.20	4.17	3.92	4.01
Congenial	3.40	3.96	4.23	3.86	4.08	3.92	3.90	4.17	4.08	4.01
Confident	3.60	4.03	3.97	3.83	4.04	3.38	3.80	4.00	4.31	3.97
Self-assured	2.80	3.98	3.86	3.82	4.06	3.31	3.90	3.83	4.08	3.90
Organized	3.20	3.96	3.75	3.91	3.98	3.46	3.90	3.83	3.62	3.86
Flexible	4.00	3.80	4.00	3.91	3.96	3.38	3.880	4.00	3.69	3.85
Assertive	3.40	3.90	3.69	3.83	3.81	3.69	4.00	3.67	3.92	3.82

Table 19 *(continued)*

Descriptive	Arts	Bus.	Educ.	Gov't.	Hlth.Sv.	Legal	Media	Rel.	Non-Tr.	Total
Ambitious	4.00	3.87	3.60	3.91	3.81	3.77	3.80	3.17	3.69	3.79
Analytic	4.00	3.66	3.72	4.04	3.71	3.69	4.20	4.17	4.15	3.78
Competitive	3.80	3.81	3.33	3.48	3.44	3.62	3.70	2.67	3.92	3.60
Patient	3.00	3.21	3.81	3.23	3.54	3.15	3.40	4.17	3.69	3.42
Academically oriented	3.80	3.27	3.97	3.57	3.25	3.31	3.10	3.83	3.23	3.41
Calm	3.60	3.24	3.57	3.23	3.56	3.15	3.50	4.17	3.15	3.39
Aggressive	3.00	3.36	2.89	3.36	3.02	3.33	2.80	2.33	3.46	3.17
Ruthless	1.80	1.58	1.43	1.82	1.71	1.62	1.90	1.17	1.54	1.61

Table 20
Self-descriptive Words by Occupational Category (Six Most Commonly Chosen Descriptive Words, and Means, by Occupational Category)

Order of Choice	Arts		Business		Education	
1	Responsible	5.00	Responsible	4.60	Responsible	4.61
2	Competent	4.80	Hardworking	4.48	Sincere	4.50
3	Hardworking	4.80	Competent	4.41	Perseverence	4.49
4	Committed	4.60	Peseverence	4.36	Committed	4.47
5	Sincere	4.60	Sincere	4.36	Competent	4.42
6	Motivated	4.60	Action oriented	4.36	Enthusiastic	4.40

Order of Choice	Government		Health Services		Legal	
1	Responsible	4.77	Responsible	4.65	Responsible	4.62
2	Action oriented	4.61	Committed	4.44	Person oriented	4.31
3	Committed	4.45	Perseverence	4.44	Hardworking	4.23
4	Motivated	4.45	Hardworking	4.44	Motivated	4.23
5	Competent	4.43	Action oriented	4.44	Challenged	4.23
6	Hardworking	4.35	Sincere	4.42	Competent	4.15

Table 20 (*continued*)

Order of Choice	Media		Religion		Non-traditional	
1	Competent	4.70	Person oriented	4.67	Responsible	4.62
2	Committed	4.60	Committed	4.67	Enthusiastic	4.46
3	Person oriented	4.60	Empathetic	4.67	Competent	4.31
4	Responsible	4.50	Sincere	4.67	Confident	4.31
5	Enthusiastic	4.40	Enthusiastic	4.50	Warm	4.31
6	Sincere	4.40	Warm	4.50	Sincere	4.23

Table 21
Self-esteem and Achievement/Motivation Correlations with
Perception of Success, Financial Compensation Satisfaction,
and Emotional Compensation Satisfaction

	Perception of Success	Financial Compensation Satisfaction	Emotional Compensation Satisfaction
Self-esteem	.3687*	.0199	.2859*
Achievement Motivation	.0575	.0486	.0239

*Significant at .001 level; n = 229.

Table 22
Self-esteem and Achievement/Motivation Correlations
with Income and Age

	Annual Income	Age
Self-esteem	.1089	.0388
Achievement Motivation	.1399	.0801

n = 229

Table 23
Factor Analysis of Self-esteem and Achievement/
Motivation (Loadings of Questions on Self-esteem
and Achievement/Motivation)

Questions	Self-esteem Factor	Achievement Motivation Factor	Discouraged Factor
Question 12	.77		
Question 13	.76		
Question 14	.68		
Question 15	.50		
Question 16	.54		
Question 17	.74		
Question 18	.70		
Question 19	.60		.41
Question 20	.45		.45
Question 21	.63		
Question 22		.74	
Question 23		.49	
Question 24		.71	
Question 25		.42	.62
Question 26		.60	
Question 27		.74	
Question 28			.71

Table 24
Factor Analysis of Self-descriptive Words (Loadings of Self-descriptive Words by Identified Factor)

Self-Descriptive Word	Factor 1	2	3	4	5	6	7	8
Knowledgeable						.66		
Competent			.60					
Academically oriented						.61		
Action oriented	.56							
Intelligent						.70		
Hardworking			.42	.44				
Competitive	.69							
Analytic								.65
High achiever	.66							
Confident	.63							
Ambitious	.74							
Self-assured	.58							
Assertive	.72							
Flexible		.40	.46					
Goal oriented	.57							
Committed				.72				
Perseverance	.33			.34				.34
Motivated				.74				
Enthusiastic	.41	.51						
Challenged				.69				
Warm		.79						
Empathetic		.64		.38				
Kind		.74						
Sincere		.58						

Table 24 *(continued)*

Self-Descriptive Word	Factor							
	1	2	3	4	5	6	7	8
Calm			.36		.72			
Patient					.77			
Congenial		.63			.42			
Optimistic	.34	.31			.32			.50
Mature		.40	.54					
Realistic			.59		.36			
Levelheaded			.66					
Organized			.69					
Leader	.54							
Openminded		.56	.35					
Ruthless							.62	
Aggressive	.64						.43	
Person oriented		.69						
Responsible			.57	.36				

Table 25
Self-descriptive Word Orientation Factors (Loadings of Descriptive Words by Factors and Variances)

Factor 1	Factor 2	Factor 3	Factor 4
Achievement Oriented	Person Oriented	Work Oriented	Career Oriented
Action oriented	Flexible	Competent	Hardworking
Competitive	Enthusiastic	Hardworking	Committed
High achiever	Warm	Flexible	Perseverence
Confident	Empathetic	Calm	Motivated
Ambitious	Kind	Mature	Challenged
Self assured	Sincere	Realistic	Empathetic
Assertive	Congenial	Level headed	Responsible
Goal oriented	Optimistic	Organized	
Perseverence	Mature	Open-minded	
Enthusiastic	Open minded	Responsible	
Optimistic	Person oriented		
Leader			
Aggressive			

Table 25 *(continued)*

Factor 5	Factor 6	Factor 7	Factor 8
Congenial Oriented	Cognitive Oriented	Forceful Oriented	Investigative Oriented
Calm	Knowledgeable	Ruthless	Analytic
Patient	Academically oriented	Aggressive	Perseverence
Congenial	Intelligent		Optimistic
Optimistic			
Realistic			
Levelheaded			

Table 26
Individual Written Definitions of Success (Number of
Respondents by Individual Definition of Success)

Individual Definition Categories	Frequency	Percent
Achieving personal goals	36	14.5
Contributing to society and/or others	29	11.6
Doing a good job, doing my best	21	8.4
Enjoying my work	14	5.6
Being happy and content	14	5.6
Receiving recognition	13	5.2
Having a balanced life	11	4.4
Achieving competence	8	3.2
Accomplishing	8	3.2
Being respected by others	7	2.8
Having freedom and independence	7	2.8
Achieving a high position	6	2.4
Marriage and family	6	2.4
Continual learning	5	2.0
Personal growth	4	1.6
Being of service to others	4	1.6
Having a lot of money	3	1.2
Receiving approval from others	2	.8
Surviving in business	1	.4

n = 199   Cumulative

% = 79.9

Table 27

Profile of Career Women Interviewed (Means and Percentages of Interviewees' Demographic Characteristics)

Profile	Means and Averages	Percent
Number of years in their field	17.6	
Age	45.1	
Ordinal position (oldest and youngest)		60.0
Anglo ethnic		78.0
Number of children	1.4	
Marital status - married		60.0
Have had mentor		65.0
Provide own and/or family's financial support		52.0
Definition of success: Achieving personal goals		52.0
Rank self well above average success (8 or better)		65.0

n = 23

Table 28
**Career Entry Decision (Method of Career Entry Decision
by Frequencies)**

Category	Frequency	Percent
Traditional - societal or family	6	26.0
By accident	5	21.7
Looking for something challenging	4	17.0
High school volunteer experience	2	8.6
Economic necessity	2	8.6
Death of a spouse	1	4.0
Self-fulfillment	1	4.0
Strong social atmosphere	1	4.0

Table 29
Career Patterns (Categorized by Frequency)

Category	Frequency	Percent
Continuous field, planned entry	8	35.0
Continuous field, unplanned entry, upwardly mobile	6	26.0
Continuous field, unplanned entry	3	13.0
Re-entry from homemaking	3	13.0
Career change	3	13.0

n = 23

Table 30
Factors Helpful in Career (by Frequency of Mention)

Helpful Factor	Frequency
Mentors	11
Personal Characteristics	9
Influence or expectations of parents	7
College professor	3
Friends	3
Meeting challenges	2
Continued personal growth	2
Enjoying work	2
Supportive/encouraging husband	2
Women's movement	2
Having full responsibility for family	2
High school counselor	1

Table 31
Perceived Characteristics of Successful Career Women
(by Frequency of Mention)

Characteristics	Frequency
Achiever, having strong drive	6
Self-confident	5
Setting goals	5
Organized	4
Self-directed	4
Contributing to/helping others	4
Energetic	3
Involved	3
Positive outlook	3
Risk taker	3

Table 31 *(continued)*

Characteristic	Frequency
Perseverance	2
Hardworking	2
Desiring to make changes	2
Have supportive spouse	2
Knowledgeable	1
Decision maker	1
Tough	1
Focused	1
Meets challenges	1
Enthusiastic	1
Fair	1
Honest	1
Intelligent	1
Encouraging	1
Agreeable	1
Androgynous	1
Enjoys her work	1
Politically aware	1
Determined	1
Analytical	1
Ambitious	1

Table 32
Self-rating of Success (by Frequency)

Level of Success	Frequency	Percent
10	2	8.6
9	2	8.6
8	11	48.0
7	4	17.0
6	2	8.6
5	2	8.6

Table 33
Interview Definitions of Career Success (by Frequency)

Definition of Success	Frequency
Achieving personal goals	12
Enjoying work	11
Achieving self-satisfaction	5
Receiving peer or community recognition	4
Making change, having an impact	4
Having plenty of money	3
Contributing to community	2
Helping others	2
Having autonomy	2
Having job security	1
Running a business - longevity	1
Being a role model	1
Breaking barriers (traditional, male oriented)	1
Having variety	1
Having a good family life	1

Table 34
Advice to Aspiring Women (by Frequency)

Statements of Advice	Frequency
Know yourself, know what you want	15
Prepare yourself, get necessary credentials	13
Promote yourself and your work	8
Work hard	6
Love what you do	5
Keep your life balanced	5
Believe in yourself	4
Volunteer to gain experience and knowledge	4
Be assertive	3
Be realistic	3
Become involved with the decision-making (organizational)	2
Know the rules	2
Be willing to take risks	2
Set goals	2
Be patient	1
Get good foundation in math and science	1

Chapter 5

Summary, Discussion, and Recommendations

The existing literature on successful career women has generally been limited to specific groups of career women in positions of high visibility and prestige, such as lawyers, physicians, and executives. Most of the research has compared career women to men, to homemakers, or to college students, rather than comparing career women with each other as a unique group in their own right.

The rationale for this study rests on these assumptions: that successful career women have characteristics in common with each other and across career fields; and that any differences among them are attributable to the specific variables identified herein.

The twin purposes of this study were to investigate the personal characteristics that successful career women have in common and to investigate any differences in self-esteem and achievement/motivation in terms of the variables of occupational field, ordinal position, age, income level, ethnic group, and career level. Hypotheses were developed to address the areas of expected differences and commonality of the successful career women.

SAMPLE GROUP

A total of 528 successful career women were identified from information provided by businesses, agencies, civic clubs, and organizations. Of this identified population, 249 career women responded with usable questionnaires, providing the information upon which this study was based. Additionally, 23 of the 25 women who were randomly selected from the questionnaire sample agreed to participate in a personal interview, providing in-depth information about the successful career women.

MEASUREMENT

The Career Woman Questionnaire was composed of 34 questions. It contained ten self-esteem measures (Rosenberg 1965); seven achievement/motivation measures adapted from the educational model, Myers' achievement/motivation scale (Myers 1965); 38 self-descriptive words (Zimmerman 1983); twelve definitions of success, to be ranked; one open-ended query about the respondents' definitions of success; and questions designed to provide demographic data. The Career Woman Interview questions provided information on career paths, components of career success, family of origin characteristics and environment, personal characteristics, career evaluation, self-reported achievement/motivation, mentoring, and other descriptive narrative.

FINDINGS—HYPOTHESIS ONE

The first hypothesis—*successful career women will have a high degree of self-esteem as measured by Rosenberg's self-esteem scale*— was supported. The overall mean for self-esteem of the successful career women was 3.49 out of a possible 4.0.

The criterion for selection for this study required that the subjects had been publicly recognized by their peers, either in the workplace or in a civic capacity, which recognition might or might not have been work-related. This external recognition itself may have contributed to the subjects' increased level of self-esteem, since it fulfilled one major component of success as defined in the literature. Public recognition and its importance to increased self-esteem supports Blotnick's (1985) estimation of the significance of recognition to persons in the workplace: "What matters is that recognition in some form is finally theirs" (p. 3).

External recognition also indicates a high degree of social

interest among the subjects since, in order to receive public recognition, they had to be involved with others. This agrees with the Adlerian assumption that success in life is related to the individual's degree of social interest. According to Miller (1986), "Women have a great desire to engage with others" (p. 140). This involvement with others—through mentors, for example— provides an external validation or support that may enhance the career woman's self-esteem. As one interviewee stated, "I'm highly motivated by people, I'm self-motivated, but people move me to act even more."

Sixty-two percent of the women studied had mentors. Based on the information provided by the interviews, these mentors had affected the women's own feelings of self-worth in terms of their careers. The following quote is an example:

My mentor seems to only give me advice when she deems it necessary, and it is something I can really use. She is a person who laughs with me and also cries with me, and boy, is she a real ego booster! She will say "You can do it" when you get maybe a little apprehensive.

The majority of the career women interviewed also identified the support and encouragement of family and friends as contributing significantly to their feelings of high self-esteem. One woman gave great credit to her grandmother, saying that "whatever I achieved in my life, I would attribute to her guidance and suggestions. . . . She always said you could achieve whatever it was you wanted to achieve."

The small degree of difference in the means of self-esteem across occupational fields also supports the concept that recognition affects self-esteem more than one's occupation does. Variety in occupational choice is more likely a function of individual interest and skills than of self-esteem.

Alternatively, the women who returned the questionnaire may have been influenced by the cover letter, which stated that she had already been "identified as a successful career woman." The overt statement of recognition of success may have positively biased the subjects, predisposing them to answer more positively than had the statement of identification of success not been included.

FINDINGS—HYPOTHESIS TWO

The second hypothesis—*successful career women as a group will have characteristics in common with successful career women within specific fields*—was supported, with the exception of the occupational field of religion.

Seven of the nine occupational fields chose the word "responsible" from the list of 38 descriptive terms as the most common word to describe themselves. The occupational field of media chose "responsible" in fourth place. Religion was the only group that did not choose "responsible" among their top 10 words, nor did they include any of the top three descriptors (for the overall group) among their top 10 words.

The comparison of self-descriptive words by occupational group showed that the religion group was followed by the non-traditional group in choosing different self-descriptive terms, which in turn was followed by the legal group. One of the legal group stated that successful career women "are hard workers, they're knowledgeable, revved up to *do something—achieve something!* . . . to change things. If they've identified something that doesn't work right they want to change it!"

It is not surprising that these three groups chose words different from those of the other occupational fields. In many respects, they could all be combined into a non-traditional category. All of these occupational fields are occupied predominantly by males. One woman stated: "I like challenges. I don't like to think that I can't do something, or that I have to seek permission from someone to do it. Don't tell me that it can't be done!" Another nontraditional woman averred that achieving a certain rank or "breaking barriers" within their career fields, "especially in things that have formerly been all male," was significant success for women.

These differences support the research findings on women in male-dominated professions, who are seen as having common characteristics, such as being more aggressive, independent, dominant, self-confident, autonomous, and unconventional (Feulner 1979; Halcomb 1979; Hennig and Jardim 1977; Keown and Keown 1982).

Alternatively, the sample for the occupational field of religion was small (n = 6), which limits drawing general conclusions about this field. This sample did not include women who had primary responsibility for a specific congregation, and that may also have contributed to their different self-description.

Another distinguishing factor may relate to the particular circumstances of the geographical location of the subjects. In the states that border Mexico, religious groups have been involved in the sanctuary movement. The community under study in particular has been very active and nationally visible in supporting this movement. This could account for their not choosing the word "responsible," which might have implied responsibility to the government or civic groups rather than responsibility to humanity.

FINDINGS—HYPOTHESIS THREE

The third hypothesis—*there will be a difference in self-esteem and achievement/motivation in terms of the variables of ordinal position, income level, and career level*—was only partially supported. Ordinal position was the only variable shown to have a significant effect on both self-esteem and achievement/motivation.

The youngest ordinal position differed significantly from and had a higher level of self-esteem than both the only and oldest ordinal positions. External recognition may be more important to the youngest ordinal position, compared to the only and oldest ordinal positions. Further breakdown of the ordinal position information indicated that the youngest ordinals with the highest levels of self-esteem were those who were the second of two; most of these had an older male sibling.

The only child ordinal position had a significant effect on achievement/motivation. This position had a higher level of achievement/motivation than any other.

Typically, the only child will compare herself with her parents; in doing so, she sets higher expectations of herself than those ordinal positions that compare themselves with their siblings. Additionally, only children tend to rely heavily on the approval of their parents and strive to live up to parental expectations. Conversely, parental expectations tend to be higher for only children than for other ordinal positions. One woman noted that "Hard work . . . is the measure of my family." Another replied that "Both [parents] agreed that I should work hard, that I should do jobs well, do tasks well."

The results of analysis of income level on achievement/motivation indicate no significant main effect. There was, however, a trend toward significance of income level on achievement/motivation. The three highest income groups had the highest levels of achievement/motivation, but the lowest mean of achievement/motivation was held by the middle group (those who earned between $41,000-60,000).

While no allowance was made for the statistical relationship of self-esteem to sibling gender, additional investigation showed that there was a noticeable number of the second-of-two youngest ordinals who had a male sibling. In such a family configuration—two children, one of each gender—there tends to be a representation of "oldest" characteristics for both siblings (Falbo 1981; Forer 1977; Jordan et al. 1982). This may have contributed to the increased self-esteem of these women, particularly if the older sibling provided encouragement and positive modeling. In the interviewing process, several of the career women identified their older brothers as having been very supportive and encouraging. These older brothers were specified as having had a considerable positive influence on the career women's early growth and development.

Labor market statistics in Arizona usually report that less than 10 percent of women employed full-time outside the home earn more than $20,000 per year. Given these statistics, it is conceivable that those women who were in the middle income category, $41,000-60,000, felt very satisfied with their income level. Although there was no statistically significant effect, this level of satisfaction could account for the positive trend. In fact, based on the interview information gathered, it is possible that these women were earning more than they had ever imagined.

The lack of statistical support for income level having an effect on self-esteem can also be understood by examining the career women's definitions of success. Their definitions of success were sought in three different ways: through a ranked list, in a written definition, and in personal interviews. The definition "achieving a very high salary" consistently ranked well below the halfway mark of all definitions of success. These women did not define the amount of money they earned as affecting their level of self-esteem. One subject wrote: "Professional success is but one part of my equation for personal happiness. Professional success is measured in recognition by others, less so by money and what it can buy."

Frieze et al. (1978) contends that women define success differently from men. The career women interviewed defined success more in terms of relationships with others, through their work, families, or community. It is therefore understandable that income had less impact on self-esteem for women than other, more person-oriented factors.

Statistical support was lacking for the idea that career level, management or nonmanagement, had an effect on self-esteem or achievement/motivation. This may have been a function of the women's lack of expectation of success (defined as management positions) rather than a specific lack of achievement/motivation (White et al. 1981). It can also be explained by again reviewing how these women defined success. In two of the three ways in which they defined success, "achieving one's personal goals" ranked highest. While personal goals can incorporate a variety of ideals, the ranking of the other definitions suggests that continually aspiring to management or higher positions is not a major goal of most of these successful career women. The fact that 72 percent of these women were already in management positions may also have influenced this finding.

Further, "receiving recognition" was among the top five definitions in all three measures. Additionally, "enjoying one's work" and "contributing to society, to others" were among the top five ranks in two of the three measures. One woman defined success as: "Accomplishing goals. Knowing that what you do makes a difference. Doing something worthwhile very well and receiving recognition for your accomplishments."

Thus, the successful career women in this study seemed to define themselves and their success in relation to their own goals as well as to their relation with others, rather than by any position of status or high income. This underscores the likelihood that women do indeed define success and achievement differently

from men. This could account for the lack of statistical significance of any effect of income or career level on the self-esteem
and achievement/motivation for successful career women.

FINDINGS—HYPOTHESIS FOUR

The fourth hypothesis—*there will be no difference in achieve-
ment/motivation and self-esteem between occupational fields or
between ethnic groups*—was statistically supported. There was
no difference among ethnic groups in self-esteem or achieve-
ment/motivation. This was expected for several reasons. First,
all of the women shared the common element of recognition. In
addition, the community from which the population was drawn
was distinctly cross-cultural, so a blending of the cultures or the
acculturation of the population was expected.

There was no *statistical* difference among occupational fields
in terms of achievement/motivation or self-esteem, but the levels
of self-esteem by occupational fields varied slightly. In other
words, all of the occupational fields had a high level of self-
esteem, although some fields were higher than others. The two
occupational groups with the highest self-esteem means were
the nontraditional (3.66) and the health services (3.58). The occupational group with the lowest self-esteem mean was the legal
group (3.20).

According to the literature, career women in nontraditional
occupations have several personal characteristics in common, including a high level of self-confidence. The nontraditional
women described themselves as more confident than any other
occupational group. The health services group included medical
doctors and psychologists, which have both generally been categorized as nontraditional occupations. This group fits into a
major component of the definition of success as identified by the
total study population—contributing to society or to others.

In the literature, the legal career women are often included in
the nontraditional category, so it is puzzling to note the discrep-
ancy in their level of self-esteem. The predominant ordinal position may have been a factor in the small difference in level of
self-esteem in this occupational category. Nevertheless, it re-

mains an unanswered question. Even though the difference is very small, it may prove worthy of further exploration.

FINDINGS—HYPOTHESIS FIVE

The fifth hypothesis—*there will be a positive relationship between self-esteem and achievement/motivation scores and the variables of perception of success, financial compensation satisfaction, and emotional compensation satisfaction*—was partially supported. Those career women who stated a high degree of perceived success had higher levels of self-esteem, as did women who had a high level of emotional compensation satisfaction.

It is not surprising that career women who perceived themselves as being more than moderately successful had a higher degree of self-esteem. That the higher degree of emotional compensation satisfaction relates to high self-esteem can be explained by again referring to how these women defined success (achieving personal goals and enjoying one's work). In other words, if they were achieving their goals and enjoying their work, they would have a higher level of emotional compensation satisfaction and higher self-esteem. The level of emotional compensation satisfaction is a very individualized construct and is definitely subject to personal interpretation.

Individual perceptions of success encompass a variety of definitions and can include unstated criteria, such as recognition by peers, achieving more, and/or earning more than one had envisioned. As one interviewee said, "Well, I had no thoughts of going into management. Things like that were out of my realm of achieving expectations!"

Miller maintains that women believe that "caring for people and participating in others' development is enhancing to [their own] self-esteem" (1986, 44). One woman in management stated that successful career women "believe in what they are doing . . . and feel good to be working as a member of the team." Another described successful career women as "usually mentors, they're always helping other people. They're not afraid to share."

The literature indicates that the variables of gender, age, family, and achievement have no empirically supported evidence of effect on the level of self-esteem. Furthermore, the evidence points to the possibility of personal interpretation as an impacting variable on self-esteem (Wylie 1979; Rosenberg and Pearlin 1978; Grayson 1986).

FINDINGS—HYPOTHESIS SIX

The sixth hypothesis—*there will be no relationship between self-esteem or achievement/motivation and the variables of age or income*—was supported. There was no identifiable relationship between self-esteem or achievement/motivation and the variables of age or income.

As stated previously, age, according to the literature, has no empirical effect on self-esteem. And since hypothesis five found some support for higher levels of emotional compensation satisfaction and self-esteem, it is reasonable to expect that the variables of age and income would have no impact on the successful career woman's self-esteem. Furthermore, in the definitions of success of the career woman, money is not a factor until many other criteria have been met.

FINDINGS—SUMMARY OF DEFINITIONS OF SUCCESS

The three measures of how the career women defined success indicated that the number one component of success was "achieving one's personal goals." The second strongest component was "receiving recognition from others." The third-place definition was divided between "enjoying one's work" and "contributing to others, to the community, and so forth."

It is interesting to note that, in all of the measures of defining success, the specific issue of money was not addressed by this population until many other criteria were met. It is possible that the issue of money was a very personal one that was not readily discussed; it may also have been included in the first definition of achieving one's goals. It is more likely, however, that the issue of money truly has less importance for women in their ordering of values. One woman identified career success as "contributing the most I can," while another pinpointed "being a good role model for younger women; having the ability to get along with the people I work with; and [receiving some] recognition for my efforts." These women seem to place a higher value on their personal satisfaction by contributing to the betterment of society, rather than on earning the highest salary. This possibility certainly presents its own problems.

According to Miller, women are consciously creating their own definitions of what constitutes success and they "are struggling to create for themselves a new concept of personhood" (1986, 44). One woman identified success as "having an impact . . . having developed some excellent skills in working with people, and . . . making some excellent decisions whenever there was a fork in the road. I always chose the [area] that had huge risks for me . . . and it's worked out very well."

FINDINGS—ACHIEVEMENT/MOTIVATION

The lack of statistical support for any relationship to achievement/motivation was initially puzzling. The assumption was made that the measures used, an adaptation of Myers' educational model, was an inappropriate measure for the achievement/motivation of women.

The lack of support for the variables of perception of success, financial compensation satisfaction, and emotional compensation satisfaction having an effect on achievement/motivation probably derives from the likelihood that women define achievement/motivation differently from men. The literature discusses the inappropriateness of attempting to transfer the research on achievement/motivation of males to females (Horner 1972; Stein and Bailey 1973; Nieva and Gutek 1981). The fact that none of the variables had any statistically significant effect for these successful career women supports the conclusions found in the literature.

The words that the career women chose to describe themselves were factor analyzed and loaded into eight factors. The factors were labeled according to the constructs that they seemed to measure. The first factor was labeled achievement-oriented, and the third factor was labeled work-oriented. The measures used in the questionnaire seemed to measure work rather than achievement/motivation. This finding implies that achievement/motivation was something separate from work for these career women.

FINDINGS—CAREER ENTRY

The career women who were interviewed illustrated some interesting patterns in how they got into their career fields. The vast majority either started in a traditional female occupation or entered by "default." When asked how they decided to enter their career field, they gave various answers, including: "There weren't as many opportunities for women in my day as there are now, and [my parents] persuaded me to go to this small state teachers college. You know, nursing and teaching were about it, then"; "Well, when the youngest child went to kindergarten, I started looking around for some kind of employment"; "just by accident"; "by chance"; "there was no plan there, [I had to] just go out and get a job in an office"; and "When I was in high school [I was asked] to volunteer my summer working at the hospital; . . . based on that, I decided that's what I truly wanted to do." Only five of the 23 interviewed had planned specifically for their careers. Four of these five were in professional careers requiring a specific level of education. These fields were medicine, law, and engineering.

The majority pattern for these career women illustrates the findings of the literature about differences in career development and choice as affected by gender. Although the women's movement has been "the most influential force of this century" (Fitzgerald and Betz 1984, 137), the career entry patterns of these women remain largely unchanged.

The women who were interviewed ranged in age from 31 to 67. Even with an age span of 36 years, it was interesting to note how similarly and traditionally these women had been socialized. There were, however, three notable exceptions, and each of these three women were in nontraditional careers. Howe maintains that the acknowledgement of the differences among individuals or between sexes is important and contends that "we may learn from the study of differences as much as we learn from similarities" (1973, 113). Therefore, the differences in career patterns for women do not need to be viewed as deviant, but can be explained as meeting different needs. The patterns are likely a function of differences in gender and in socialization.

One influencing factor in the ultimate career choice might have been the choice of which parent the young child chose to emulate and/or please. The majority of the women interviewed who were in the nontraditional fields seemed to be more closely aligned with their fathers. The exceptions to that pattern were women who had very independent and often nontraditional mothers. The significance of parental influence was frequently mentioned in the interviews. Indeed, there was more emphasis on parental influence and modeling than on the conscious choosing process. This modeling construct has been identified as an important function of career development by several theorists (Astin 1984; Holland 1973; Krumboltz 1976; Tiedeman and Miller 1984).

The literature on the career history and development of women asks many questions, identifies several variables, and finds differences between career development for men and for women. No clear, consistent pattern was found for women.

FINDINGS—GOAL SETTING

The predominant definition of success for these career women was "achieving one's personal goals." Each of the women interviewed was asked if she set goals, and, if so, what process she followed. Only nine of the 23 women stated without hesitation that they set goals. One woman stated,

I have always, I think, visualized and set goals for myself. . . . I have a philosophy of how I'm getting there. I don't set 1, 2, 3, 4 year plans . . . I'm in training now . . . [and] whenever I feel like I'm ready, that's when I will make my move! But that's how I look at it, rather than putting a year on it. . . . You never know when the opportunity will come up.

Another stated, " I set goals all the time. . . . and I set too many. I am learning to not set as many goals, and have more realistic ones." When they began their careers, however, four of these nine had no career goals. Said one, "I had no concept of goal setting in the beginning, I just worked." Six of the 23 women stated that they sometimes set goals; the remaining eight either did not set goals or said that if it happened, the process was subconscious.

The process for goal setting ranged from very specific, long-term (six to ten year) goals, to very general goals that were not formally written out. Several of the women said that their goal emphasis was changing and that they were focusing more on their families. The majority seemed to have an informal method of goal setting, when they set goals at all. One woman stated, "I guess as things occur that are of interest to me, I look to see if I can develop that further rather than planning out some kind of chain of events that I want to see happen."

Most career women were thus not clear on their process of goal setting. There seemed to be some variance between the primary definition of success as achieving one's personal goals and the fact that the women were very flexible and almost casual about setting goals. It is possible that while these women had personal goals, they were often not clearly identified. Several used the term "dream" instead of classifying their thought as a goal. This type of "soft goal setting" agrees with the information found in the literature, which suggests that successful career women generally are not rigid goal setters (Hennig and Jardim 1977; Keown and Keown 1982; Halcomb 1979; Blotnick 1985). One woman said, "I don't feel compulsive about trying to figure out where it is I'm going. I have a sense that I'm moving in some direction, and I'm comfortable allowing that to unfold."

It could also be that women tend to approach goal setting in a holistic manner that would allow for more spontaneity and balance. Based on their comments, it is clear that these career women valued balance in their lives and therefore chose flexible professional goals that could be compatible with their personal lives. These women were committed to the importance of satisfying personal relationships as well as meeting their career wants and needs. As one woman said, "It's important to have an adequate balance in my life. I think the thing that burns most people out is that your ego becomes so tied in to that one thing that you don't have anything else that sustains you." These women were more concerned with being unique and having their own identity, rather than with trying to fit a stereotype of goal setting for success.

SUMMARY OF FINDINGS

The strongest characteristic shared by these successful career women was a high degree of self-esteem. All occupational groups had high degrees of self-esteem, although there were slight differences (not statistically significant) in levels of self-esteem between occupational fields. Self-esteem was affected to a statistically significant degree by ordinal position. Youngest children had a higher level of self-esteem than did only or oldest children. Self-esteem also had a statistically significant relationship to the career woman's level of perceived success and emotional compensation satisfaction level. Self-esteem was not affected by age, income level, ethnic group, or career level (management or nonmanagement). These findings are, for the most part, compatible with the literature on self-esteem. The literature indicates that the variables of gender, age, family, and achievement have no effect on the level of self-esteem, and there is some consideration that personal interpretation may affect self-esteem. The one clear difference found in this study is in the effect of ordinal position on self-esteem, which highlights the importance of including information on birth order in future research on self-esteem.

The subjects chose similar self-descriptive words. These career women described themselves as responsible, competent, and hardworking. The literature indicates that some of the most common descriptive characteristics of successful career women include being hard workers and being committed to their careers. The nontraditional career women described themselves somewhat differently, as responsible, confident, and enthusiastic. Further, the literature identifies women in male-dominated professions as being more independent, self-confident, and unconventional.

The career women also tended to define success similarly. The major components of success as defined by the subjects were: (1) achieving one's personal goals, (2) receiving recognition from others, (3) enjoying one's work, and (4) contributing to others, to the community, and so forth. These definitions are not those typically identified in the literature, which included having corporate management positions, receiving a high salary, or winning power and fame.

There was no statistical support for any relationship to achievement/motivation. This indicates that the items used in the questionnaire did not measure achievement/motivation for this group. As indicated in the literature, achievement/motivation research has focused primarily on males, and the results do not seem to transfer to females. There were, however, some trends toward significance. Only children appeared to have a higher degree of achievement/motivation, as did women earning $100,000 and over.

The career women interviewed had a profile closely resembling the overall sample. The characteristic most commonly shared by these women was the lack of pre-planning for their career fields. Although they had not set specific career goals, most of the women had had some exposure (either by observation or volunteer work) to the career field that they ultimately entered. Many of the career women stated that they had entered their field "by accident," which coincides with the lack of application to women of career theories as outlined in the literature. Another common characteristic of the women interviewed was their tendency to use informal methods of goal setting, if indeed, they set goals at all. Most of them seemed comfortable with their current career situation and were in a status quo position with their goal setting.

CONCLUSIONS

The analysis of the data prompted the following conclusions about the successful career women in this study.

1. Women who have been publicly recognized by their peers have a high level of self-esteem.
2. Women have a different pattern of career development from men.

3. Women focus more on "contributing to society/to others" than on "earning a high salary."
4. Women define themselves as "hardworking" rather than as "achievement-oriented."
5. Women are generally not rigid goal setters.
6. Women define success differently from men.

LIMITATIONS

This study used subjects who were a convenient sample of career women who had been recognized by their peers in a large city in southern Arizona. A questionnaire method of measurement was used. The generalizability of this study is restricted by the sample characteristics.

RECOMMENDATIONS

Based on the findings of this study, there are numerous possibilities for continued research on career women. Several recommendations can be made.

It is recommended that studies be done to compare women who have been recognized by their peers with women who have not been so recognized. This could provide information on the value of recognition and identify similarities and differences between the two groups.

Because of a lack of statistical measurement of achievement/ motivation for these subjects, it is strongly recommended that the measurement of achievement/motivation for women be investigated. It could be most beneficial to develop an instrument that provides a more accurate measure than did the educational adaptation used in this study.

Replication of this study in other geographical locations is also recommended so that generalizations may be made to a larger segment of the population; spurious results that may have been found in this study would be unlikely to be duplicated over time and through repeated experiments.

IMPLICATIONS FOR THE PRACTITIONER

Although caution must be exercised in generalizing beyond this sample, the results suggest several implications.

The data indicate that career women who have been publicly recognized by their peers have a high level of self-esteem. This is supported by the definitions of success defined by this population, which include "recognition" as one of the top three components of success. If recognition contributes to career women's definition of their own success and to improved self-esteem, employers and organizations could construct specific opportunities to increase their recognition of women's contributions, thereby benefiting everyone involved. Women themselves can recognize this phenomenon and create opportunities for recognition both individually and in their commmunities.

These career women were more likely to perceive themselves as successful if they were achieving their own goals, enjoying their work, receiving recognition from others, and contributing to the community, or to others', well-being. They did not define the amount of money they earned as a major component of their success. While the amount of money earned may not measure success, it still remains an important factor for all lifestyles. Given the often discussed disparity in pay between males and females in the workplace, career women may choose to re-examine their definitions of success to include money as a stronger value, or to be more realistic and specific in their goal-setting practices.

Finally, career women may choose to take the advice that they gave to these women aspiring to enter their fields. They most frequently recommended to these women: "Know yourself, know what you want," "believe in yourself," "don't limit yourself, be willing to take risks," "have a passion for what you do," "prepare yourself, get the necessary credentials," and "promote yourself and your work."

Letter to Organizations

Dear

I am writing to ask your group's assistance in a research project that will provide information on career women. I am interested in the personality characteristics and demographics of successful career women.

Little research has been done on career women across all career levels and types. This is the area I propose to address. Your organization can assist in this project by providing me with a list of names, addresses, and phone numbers of the members you have nominated for special recognition in the past five years who fit the following definition: WOMEN WHO HAVE BEEN RECOGNIZED AS SUCCESSFUL BY THEIR PEERS *BY VIRTUE OF HAVING BEEN NOMINATED FOR RECOGNITION OR SELECTION* EITHER BY A PROFESSIONAL ORGANIZATION, CIVIC GROUP, WOMEN'S RECOGNITION EVENT, OR THEIR EMPLOYER. These women will be contacted for participation in the study, which will require minimal time on their part.

I am enclosing a stamped, addressed envelope for your convenience. If you have any questions or would like further information, please feel free to call my office 887-9506 or home 297-4031. Thank you for your cooperation.

Sincerely,

Cecilia A. Northcutt, Ph.D.

Questionnaire Cover Letter

Dear Career Woman,

You have been recognized as one of the successful career women in Tucson, and I am writing to ask your assistance in my research project that will provide valuable information on career women.

I am enclosing a brief questionnaire for you to complete and return to me in the addressed envelope enclosed. You will notice that there is no identification on the questionnaire, so that any information you record will be completely anonymous. Upon reading the questionnaire, should you decide that you do not care to participate, that is your choice. Your participation is completely voluntary. The information from the questionnaire is confidential and will be used for research and publication only.

The questionnaires are numbered in order for me to be able to do a random selection of women who will be asked to take part in the second phase of my project, which involves an interview.

I would appreciate your completion of the questionnaire as soon as possible. *They need to be returned by November 7, 1986.* Because you are very busy and your time is valuable, I have made every effort to keep the questionnaire as brief as possible. It should take about 20 minutes to complete.

   Thank you for your willingness to contribute to the body of
knowledge about career women.

Sincerely,

Cecilia A. Northcutt, Ph.D.

Career Women Questionnaire

You have been selected to assist in the study of successful career women. The information you provide will be kept confidential, and your anonymity is assured. This is not a test, and there are no wrong answers.

Your honest answers will be <u>deeply appreciated</u>.

1. Occupational field_____

   Job title _____

   This position is (check one) _____paid _____volunteer

   Number of years in field_____ Number of years in

   current position_____

   Currently: active_____ retired_____

   Management position yes___ no___

2. Check highest degree attained:

   high school_____   apprenticeship_____   master's_____

   associate_____   bachelor's_____   doctorate_____

   post-doctorate_____

3. Age: 25-35____   36-45____   46-55____   56-65____   65+__

4. Ordinal position in family of origin--starting with the OLDEST, list all BROTHERS AND SISTERS in your family (BE SURE TO INCLUDE YOURSELF). List number of years older or younger than you.

    Example: YOUR SIBLINGS:

1.brother +2 years older   1._____

2.ME_____   2._____

3.sister -2 years younger   3._____

4.brother-6 years younger   4._____

5.half-sister-10 years younger 5._____

                           6._____

                           7._____

                           8._____

                           9._____

5. Marital status - check one:

married_____ divorced_____ separated_____ widowed_____

re-married_____   never married_____

6. Number of children_____

7. Ethnicity: Native American_____ Asian_____ Anglo__

Other_____   Black_____   Mexican American_____

8. Mentor information:

I have or have had a mentor in my career--yes____ no____

My mentor is ____male ____female. My mentor was ___male ___female.

9. I rank my career success as:

extremely successful___ successful_____ moderate_____ unsuccessful__

10. Please RANK, IN ORDER OF IMPORTANCE, your definitions of success from the list below, using 1 as most important and 12 as least important.

_____ Becoming an authority in your occupation.

_____ Obtaining recognition from others in your job.

_____ Obtaining awards outside the organization.

_____ Obtaining recognition from friends or others outside of work.

_____ Being well liked.

_____ Contributing to the welfare of friends or personal acquaintances.

_____ Developing a strong relationship with others on the job.

_____ Supervising volunteer organizations or community projects.

_____ Achieving a very high salary.

_____ Having a title and job description indicating high responsibility.

_____ Marrying a person who has money or position.

_____ Acquiring a large home or expensive real estate.

11. Briefly, give your own definition of success.

Please respond as quickly and candidly as possible to the following items.

12. I feel that I'm a person of worth, at least on an equal plane with others.

   strongly agree___   agree___   disagree___
   strongly disagree___

13. I feel that I have a number of good qualities.

   strongly agree___   agree___   disagree___
   strongly disagree___

14. All in all, I am inclined to feel that I am a failure.

   strongly agree___   agree___   disagree___
   strongly disagree___

15. I am able to do things as well as most other people.

   strongly agree___   agree___   disagree___
   strongly disagree___

16. I feel I do not have much to be proud of.

   strongly agree___   agree___   disagree___
   strongly disagree___

17. I take a positive attitude toward myself.

   strongly agree___   agree___   disagree___
   strongly disagree___

18. On the whole, I am satisfied with myself.

   strongly agree___   agree___   disagree___

   strongly disagree___

19. I wish I could have more respect for myself.

   strongly agree___   agree___   disagree___

   strongly disagree___

20. I certainly feel useless at times.

   strongly agree___   agree___   disagree___

   strongly disagree___

21. At times I think I am no good at all.

   strongly agree___   agree___   disagree___

   strongly disagree___

22. I am a harder worker at my job than the average career

   woman.

   strongly agree___   agree___   disagree___

   strongly disagree___

23. Other workers think of me as being too serious.

   strongly agree___   agree___   disagree___

   strongly disagree___

24. Most of my superiors/supervisors/clientele think of me

   as one of their hardest workers.

   strongly agree___   agree___   disagree___

   strongly disagree___

120 Appendix C

25. Other interests (sports, hobbies, etc.) keep me from
being exemplary in my field.

strongly agree___   agree___   disagree___
strongly disagree___

26. I really want to succeed.

strongly agree___   agree___   disagree___
strongly disagree___

27. My friends think of me as a hard worker.

strongly agree___   agree___   disagree___
strongly disagree___

28. My family commitments keep me from being exemplary in
my field.

strongly agree___   agree___   disagree___
strongly disagree___

29. The words presented below are descriptive and may relate
to your career success. It is how you perceive yourself
at the present time. Please circle the appropriate number
which describes you best for each word.

1 = NOT AT ALL   2 = SLIGHTLY   3 = MODERATELY   4 = VERY
5 = EXTREMELY

1. knowledgeable   1 2 3 4 5

2. competent   1 2 3 4 5

3. academically-oriented   1 2 3 4 5

4. action-oriented   1 2 3 4 5

5.	intelligent	1	2	3	4	5
6.	hardworking	1	2	3	4	5
7.	competitive	1	2	3	4	5
8.	analytic	1	2	3	4	5
9.	high achiever	1	2	3	4	5
10.	confident	1	2	3	4	5
11.	ambitious	1	2	3	4	5
12.	self-assured	1	2	3	4	5
13.	assertive	1	2	3	4	5
14.	flexible	1	2	3	4	5
15.	goal-oriented	1	2	3	4	5
16.	committed	1	2	3	4	5
17.	persevering	1	2	3	4	5
18.	motivated	1	2	3	4	5
19.	enthusiastic	1	2	3	4	5
20.	challenged	1	2	3	4	5
21.	warm	1	2	3	4	5
22.	empathetic	1	2	3	4	5
23.	kind	1	2	3	4	5
24.	sincere	1	2	3	4	5
25.	calm	1	2	3	4	5
26.	patient	1	2	3	4	5
27.	congenial	1	2	3	4	5
28.	optimistic	1	2	3	4	5
29.	mature	1	2	3	4	5

30. realistic   1 2 3 4 5

31. levelheaded   1 2 3 4 5

32. organized   1 2 3 4 5

33. leader   1 2 3 4 5

34. openminded   1 2 3 4 5

35. ruthless   1 2 3 4 5

36. aggressive   1 2 3 4 5

37. person-oriented   1 2 3 4 5

38. responsible   1 2 3 4 5

30. Please select the ten characteristics from the above
    list that you feel   HAVE BEEN MOST INFLUENTIAL in your
    career. Rank these characteristics   with 1 being most
    important and 2 being second most important, etc.

    1st important_____

    2nd important_____

    3rd important_____

    4th important_____

    5th important_____

    6th important_____

    7th important_____

    8th important_____

    9th important_____

    10th important_____

31. I am <u>financially</u> compensated for my work:

    extremely well___   well___   adequately___   not enough__

32. I am <u>emotionally</u> compensated for my work:

    extremely well___   well___   adequately___   not enough__

33. My annual income is: up to $20,000_____ $21-40,000_____

    $41-60,000_____ $61-80,000_____ $81-100,000_____

    $101,000+_____

    Full-time___   Part-time___

34. I am supplying the primary financial support for my

    family or myself

       YES___   NO___   EQUALLY SHARED___

Interview Questions

Questions to be asked during the interview:

1. How did you decide to enter your career field?
2. Would you describe your career history for me?
3. What has been helpful to you in your career?

   Situations or events

   People

   Personal characteristics or attributes

4. Describe attributes or characteristics of career women whom you perceive to be successful.
5. What are your career goals at this point in your life?
6. Have these goals changed from your original goals? If so, how?
7. On a scale of 0 to 10, with 10 being "extremely successful," rate how successful you feel you are at this point in your career.
8. How would you define career success?
9. What advice do you have for aspiring women in your field?

References

Abi-Karam, N., and J. C. Love. 1984. *Personality Needs Profile of Some Professional Women.* Washington, D.C.: U.S. Department of Education ERIC, April.

Anastasi, A. 1982. *Psychological Testing,* 5th ed. New York: Macmillan.

Astin, H. S. 1984. "The Meaning of Work in Women's Lives: A Sociopsychological Model of Career Choice and Work Behavior." *Counseling Psychologist* 12 (4): 17-126.

Atkinson, J. W., and N. T. Feather, eds. 1974. *A Theory of Achievement Motivation.* New York: Robert E. Krieger.

Atkinson, J. W., and J. O. Raynor. 1974. *Motivation and Achievement.* Washington, D.C.: V. H. Winston & Sons.

Bachtold, L. M. 1973. "Similarities in Personality Profiles of College and Career Women." *Psychological Reports* 33: 431-436.

Bachtold, L. M. 1976. "Personality Characteristics of Women of Distinction." *Psychology of Women Quarterly* 1 (1): 70-78.

Baker, M. 1985. "Career Women and Self-Concept." *International Journal of Women's Studies* 8 (3): 214-227.

Bandura, A. 1969. *Principles of Behavior Modification.* New York: Holt, Rinehart and Winston.

Bloom, D. E. 1986. "Women and Work." *American Demographics* September: 25-30.

Blotnick, S. 1985. *Otherwise Engaged: The Private Lives of Successful Career Women.* New York: Facts on File.

Brown, L. K. 1981. *The Woman Manager in the United States: A Re-*

128 References

search Analysis and Bibliography. Washington, D.C.: BPW
Foundation.

Bureau of Labor Statistics. 1983. *Women at Work: A Chartbook*
[Bulletin 2168]. Washington, D.C.: U.S. Department of Labor.

Catalyst. 1980. *What to Do with the Rest of Your Life.* New York: Simon
and Schuster.

Christensen, O. C. 1983. "The Rationale for Family Counseling." In
Adlerian Family Counseling, ed. O. C. Christensen and T. G.
Schramski, 3-8. Minneapolis: Educational Media Corp.

Chusmir, L. H. 1985. "Motivation of Managers: Is Gender a Factor?"
Psychology of Women Quarterly. 9 (1): 153-159.

Corsini, R. J. ed. 1973. *Current Psychotherapies.* Itasca, Ill.: F. E.
Peacock.

Dreikurs, R. 1971. *Social Equality: The Challenge of Today.* Chicago:
Contemporary Books.

Dudley, G. A., and Tiedeman, D. V. 1977. *Career Development: Exploration and Commitment.* Muncie, Ind.: Accelerated Development.

Erikson, E. H. 1950. *Childhood and Society.* New York: Norton.

Falbo, T. 1981. "Relationships Between Birth Category, Achievement,
and Interpersonal Orientation." *Journal of Personality and Social
Psychology* 4 (1): 121-131.

Feulner, P. N. 1979. *Women in the Professions: A Social-Psychological
Study.* Palo Alto, Calif.: R & E Research Associates.

Fitzgerald, L. F., and N. E. Betz. 1983. "Issues in the Vocational Psychology of Women." In *Handbook of Vocational Psychology,* Vol. 1,
ed. W. B. Walsch and S. H. Osipow. Hillsdale, N.J.: Earlbaum
Associates.

Forer, L. K. 1977. *The Birth Order Factor.* New York: Pocket Books.

Fox, M. F., and S. Hesse-Biber. 1984. *Women at Work.* Mountain View,
Calif.: Mayfield.

Fredrickson, R. H. 1982. *Career Information.* Englewood Cliffs, N.J.:
Prentice-Hall.

Frieze, I. H., J. E. Parsons, P. B. Johnson, D. N. Ruble, and G. L. Zell-
man. 1978. *Women and Sex Roles—A Social Psychological Perspective.* New York: W. W. Norton.

Gay, L. R. 1976. *Educational Research—Competencies for Analysis and
Application.* Columbus, Ohio: Charles E. Merrill.

Gilbert, L. A. 1984. "Comments on the Meaning of Work in Women's
Lives." *Counseling Psychologist* 12 (4): 129.

Ginzberg, E., S. W. Ginsburg, S. Axelrad, and J. L. Herma. 1951.
Occupational Choice: An Approach to a General Theory. New
York: Columbia University Press.

Glass, G. V., and K. D. Hopkins. 1984. *Statistical Methods in Education* and *Psychology,* 2nd ed. Englewood Cliffs, N.J.: Prentice-Hall.

Grayson, P. A. 1986. "Disavowing the Past: A Maneuver to Protect Self-Esteem." *Individual Psychology: The Journal of Adlerian Theory, Research and Practice* 42 (3): 330-338.

Halcomb, R. 1979. *Women Making It.* New York: Atheneum.

Harlan, A., and C. Weiss. 1981. *Moving Up: Women in Managerial Careers, Final Report.* Center for Research on Women, Wellesley College, working paper no. 86.

Helson, R. 1972. "The Changing Image of the Career Woman." *Journal of Social Issues* 28 (2): 33-46.

Hennig, M., and A. Jardim. 1977. *The Managerial Woman.* New York: Anchor Press.

Hjelle, L. A., and D. J. Ziegler. 1981. *Personality Theories—Basic Assumptions, Research, and Applications,* 2nd ed. New York: McGraw-Hill.

Holland, J. L. 1973. *Making Vocational Choices: A Theory of Careers.* Englewood Cliffs, N.J.: Prentice-Hall.

Horner, M. S. 1972. "Toward an Understanding of Achievement-Related Conflicts in Women." *Journal of Social Issues* 28 (2): 157-175.

Horton, J.A. 1975. "The Personality Characteristics of Professional Career Women: A Study of the Concurrent Validity of John Holland's Theory of Vocational Choice." Ph.D. diss. Ohio State University.

Howe, F. 1973. "Sexual Stereotypes and the Public Schools." In "Successful Women in the Sciences: An Analysis of Determinants," ed. R. B. Kundsin. *Annals of the New York Academy of Sciences* 208 (March 15): 109-114.

Jordan, E. W., M. M. Whiteside, and G. J. Manaster. 1982. "A Practical and Effective Research Measure of Birth Order." *Individual Psychology: The Journal of Adlerian Theory, Research and Practice* 38 (3): 253-260.

Kagan, J. 1972. "The Emergence of Sex Differences." *School Review* 80 (2): 217-227.

Keown, A. L., and C. F. Keown. 1985. "Factors of Success for Women in Business." *International Journal of Women's Studies* 8 (3): 278-285.

Keown, C. F., and A. L. Keown. 1982. "Success Factors for Corporate Women Executives." *Group and Organization Studies* 7 (4): 445-456.

Krumboltz, J. D., and R. B. Baker. 1973. "Behavioral Counseling for Vocational Decisions." In *Career Guidance for a New Age,* ed. H. Borrow. Boston: Houghton-Mifflin.

Krumboltz, J. D., A. M. Mitchell, and G. B. Jones. 1976. "A Social Learning Theory of Career Selection." *Counseling Psychologist* 6 (1): 71-81.

Kundsin, R. B., ed. 1973. "Successful Women in the Sciences: An Analysis of Determinants." *Annals of the New York Academy of Sciences* 208 (March 15).

Manaster, G. J., and R. J. Corsini. 1982. *Individual Psychology Theory and Practice.* Itasca, Ill.: F. E. Peacock.

Maslow, A. H. 1954. *Motivation and Personality.* New York: Harper & Row.

Miller, J. B. 1986. *Toward a New Psychology of Women,* 2nd ed. Boston: Beacon Press.

Miller-Tiedeman, A. L., and M. Niemi. 1977. *An "I" Power Primer: Part Two, Structuring Another's Responsibility into His or Her Action.* Focus on Guidance, 9 (8).

Miller-Tiedeman, A. L., and D. V. Tiedeman. 1982. *Career Development: Journey into Personal Power.* Schenectady, N.Y.: Character Research Press.

Mitchell, A. M., G. B. Jones, and J. D. Krumboltz. 1979. *Social Learning and Career Decision Making.* Cranston, R.I.: Carroll Press.

Morris, E. F. 1974. "The Personality Traits and Psychological Needs of Educated Homemakers and Career Women." Ed.D. diss. Arizona State University.

Mosak, H. H., and R. Dreikurs. 1973. "Adlerian Psychotherapy." In *Current Psychotherapies,* ed. R. J. Corsini, 35-83. Itasca, Ill.: F. E. Peacock.

Myers, A. E. 1965. "Risktaking and Academic Success and Their Relation to an Objective Measure of Achievement Motivation." *Educational and Psychological Measurement* 25: 355-363.

Nieva, V. F., and B. A. Gutek. 1981. *Women and Work—a Psychological Perspective.* New York: Praeger.

Osipow, S. H. 1973. *Theories of Career Development.* Englewood Cliffs, N.J.: Prentice-Hall.

Osipow, S. H. 1983. *Theories of Career Development,* 3rd ed. Englewood Cliffs, N.J.: Prentice-Hall.

Peatling, J. H., and D. V. Tiedeman. 1977. *Career Development: Designing Self.* Muncie, Ind.: Accelerated Development.

Pinkstaff, M. A., and A. B. Wilkinson. 1979. *Women at Work: Overcoming the Obstacles.* Menlo Park, Calif.: Addison-Wesley.

Powers, S., and M. J. Wagner. 1984a. "Regression Analysis of Achievement Motivation." *The Journal of Psychology* 117: 273-276.

Powers, S., and M. J. Wagner. 1984b. "Attributions for School Achievement of Middle School Students." *Journal of Early Adolescence* 4 (3): 215-222.

Pryor, M. G., and J. B. Reeves. 1982. "Male and Female Patterns of Work Opportunity Structure and Life Satisfaction." *International Journal of Women's Studies* 5 (3): 215-226.

Rosenberg, M. 1965. *Society and the Adolescent Self-Image.* Princeton, N.J.: Princeton University Press.

Rosenberg, M., and L. I. Pearlin. 1978. "Social Class and Self-Esteem among Children and Adults." *American Journal of Sociology* 84 (1): 53-75.

Ruddick, S., and P. Daniels, eds. 1977. *Working It Out.* New York: Pantheon.

Shaevitz, M. H. 1984. *The Superwoman Syndrome.* New York: Warner Books.

Snell, W. E., Jr., L. Hargrove, and T. Falbo. 1986. "Birth Order and Achievement Motivation Configurations in Women and Men." *Individual Psychology: The Journal of Adlerian Theory, Research and Practice* 42 (3): 428-438.

Stein, A. H., and M. M. Bailey. 1973. "The Socialization of Achievement Orientation in Females." *Psychological Bulletin* 80 (5): 345-366.

Super, D., R. Starishevsky, N. Matlin, and J. P. Jordann. 1963. *Career Development: Self-Concept Theory.* Princeton, N.J.: College Entrance Examination Board.

Temmen, K. 1982. *A Research Study of Selected Successful Women Administrators in the Educational Field.* St. Louis: CEMREL.

Thomas, C. R., and Marchant, W. C. 1983. "Basic Principles of Adlerian Family Counseling." In *Adlerian Family Counseling,* ed. O. C. Christensen and T. G. Schramski, 9-26. Minneapolis: Educational Media Corporation.

Tiedeman, D. V., and A. L. Miller-Tiedeman. 1977. In *"I" Power Primer: Part One: Structure and Its Enablement of Interaction.* Focus on Guidance, 9 (7).

Tiedeman, D. V., and A. L. Miller-Tiedeman. 1984. "Career Decision-Making: An Individualistic Perspective." In *Career Choice and Development,* ed. D. Brown and L. Brooks. San Francisco: Jossey-Bass.

Tiedeman, D. V., and R. P. O'Hara. 1963. *Career Development: Choice and Adjustment.* Princeton, N.J.: College Entrance Examination Board.

Tobias, S. 1978. *Overcoming Math Anxiety.* New York: W. W. Norton.

Trahey, J. 1977. *On Women and Power: Who's Got It? How to Get It?* New York: Rawson Associates.

Waddell, F. T. 1982. "Factors Affecting Choice, Satisfaction and Success in the Female Self-Employed." *Journal of Vocational Behavior* 23: 294-304.

Wagner, M. J., S. Powers, and P. Irwin. 1985. "The Prediction of Achievement Motivation Using Performance Attributional Variables." *Journal of Psychology* 119 (6): 595-598.

Walsh, W. B., and S. H. Osipow, eds. 1983. *Handbook of Vocational Psychology. Volume 1: Foundations.* Hillsdale, N.J.: Lawrence Erlbaum Associates.

Weiner, B. 1985. *Human Motivation.* New York: Springer-Verlag.

White, M. C., G. DeSanctis, and M. D. Crino. 1981. "Achievement, Self-Confidence, Personality Traits and Leadership Ability: A Review of the Literature on Sex Differences." *Psychological Reports* 48: 547-569.

Williams, S. W., and J. C. McCullers. 1983. "Personal Factors Related to Typicalness of Career and Success in Active Professional Women." *Psychology of Women Quarterly* 7 (4): 343-357.

Wood, M. M., and S. T. Greenfeld. 1978. "Meaning of Success: A Comparison of Attitudes among Women in Male-Dominated and Female-Dominated Occupations." Paper presented at annual meeting of the American Psychological Association, August 28.

Wylie, R. C. 1979. *The Self Concept,* vol. 2, rev. ed. Lincoln, Neb.: University of Nebraska Press.

Yogev, S. 1983. "Judging the Professional Woman: Changing Research, Changing Values." *Psychology of Women Quarterly* 7 (3): 219-234.

Zimmerman, L. M. 1983. *Factors Influencing Career Success of Women in Nursing.* Ph.D. diss., University of Nebraska.

Zunker, V. G. 1986. *Career Counseling: Applied Concepts of Life Planning,* 2nd ed. Monterey, Calif.: Brooks/Cole.

Index

Recognition, 5, 6, 26, 28, 40, 41,
49, 55, 60, 69, 85, 90, 94, 95,
97, 99, 100, 101, 102, 103, 107,
109, 110, 111, 113, 117
Reinforcement, 18, 23
Relationships, 4, 10, 24, 37, 38,
39, 45, 46, 54, 61, 69, 98, 99,
101, 103, 106, 107, 108
Research hypotheses, 7, 20, 44,
47
Responsible, 2, 20, 26, 30, 34, 36,
49, 50, 51, 58, 69, 70, 82, 88,
96, 97, 107, 117, 122
Risk-takers, 30, 59, 88
Roe, A., 9, 10, 22
Rosenberg, M., 5, 38, 39, 42, 44,
50, 51, 94, 102

Salaries, 26, 28, 69, 98, 103, 108,
109, 117, 123
Sample groups, 8, 41, 42, 43, 47,
48, 55, 93, 94, 96, 97, 108, 109,
110
Self-confident, 30, 31, 59, 88, 96,
100, 107
Self-descriptive, 50, 51, 52, 55,
70, 81, 96, 97, 107, 120
Self-esteem, 2, 3, 4, 5, 6, 7, 8, 26,
29, 38, 39, 40, 41, 42, 43, 44,
45, 46, 50, 51, 52, 53, 54, 55,
61, 79, 80, 93, 94, 95, 97, 98,
99, 100, 101, 102, 107, 108, 110
Sex-role stereotyping, 21, 22, 31

Social interest, 25, 28, 94, 95
Socialization, 3, 20, 22, 40, 56,
105
Successful career women, 1, 2, 3,
4, 5, 6, 8, 25, 26, 28, 30, 31,
39, 40, 41, 42, 44, 45, 47, 51,
55, 58, 59, 60, 61, 68, 93, 94,
99, 100, 101, 103, 106, 107,
108, 111, 113, 115, 125
Successful women managers, 3,
27, 29
Super, D., 8, 9, 10, 11, 12, 13, 16

Tiedeman, D. V., and R. P.
O'Hara, 13, 14, 15, 16, 17, 19,
105

Unplanned career, 58, 87
Upwardly mobile career, 57, 87

Vocational choices, 8, 9, 10, 11,
12, 14, 18, 20

Williams, S. W., and J. C.
McCullers, 27, 34
Wood, M. M., and S. T. Green-
feld, 9, 23, 26
Wylie, R. C., 38, 39, 102

Zimmerman, L. M., 30, 42, 94
Zunker, V. G., 8, 9, 10, 11, 12,
13, 14, 15, 16, 17, 18, 19

About the Author

CECILIA ANN NORTHCUTT is a psychologist in private practice. She has authored curriculum and instructional materials for the Arizona Department of Education and the Arizona Department of Corrections, as well as articles published in *Career Education Quarterly* and *Arizona Personnel and Guidance Journal.*